how it can be and is being done in our world today. Jeff talks the talk and walks the walk—he knows what it is to feel good, be good, and do good."

—**Kartar Khalsa,** CEO Golden Temple Natural Foods, makers of Yogi Tea and Peace Cereal

"In *Working for Good,* Jeff Klein helps us get in touch with our primary, natural purpose—which gives priority to the common good of us all."

—**Terry Mollner,** Chair of Stakeholders Capital, Co-Founder and Member of the Board of the Calvert Social Investment Funds, and Member of the Board of Ben & Jerry's

"The Working for Good model uncovers the mysterious dance between self and other, culminating in the expression of what is truly possible."

—**Bijoy Goswami,** Founder, Bootstrap Austin, and author, *The Human Fabric*

"In the new business paradigm, which manages for positive outcomes for all stakeholders, bringing your best self into the workplace is critical for individual, team, and business success. Jeff Klein's insightful book makes remarkable use of story and guided reflections to provide readers with insights on how to uncover one's best self and help co-create businesses where everyone flourishes."

—**John Mackey,** Chairman and CEO of Whole Foods Market

WORKING
for GOOD

Making a Difference
While Making a Living

WORKING
for GOOD

Jeff Klein

in collaboration with Elad Levinson
and Julie van Amerongen

SOUNDS TRUE
Boulder, Colorado

Sounds True, Inc.
Boulder, CO 80306

Cover and book design by Dean Olson
Published 2009
10 9 8 7 6 5 4 3 2 1
Printed in Canada

Library of Congress Cataloging-in-Publication Data

Klein, Jeff.
  Working for good: making a difference while making a living / by Jeff Klein.
      p. cm.
  ISBN 978-1-59179-726-5
  1. Social responsibility of business. 2. Work—Social aspects. I. Title.
  HD60.K554 2009
  658.4'08—dc22

                                        2009009217

To the liberation of all beings.

Always you have been told that work is a curse and labor a misfortune. But I say to you that when you work you fulfill a part of earth's furthest dream, assigned to you when that dream was born. And in keeping yourself with labor you are in truth loving life. And to love life through labor is to be intimate with life's inmost secret.

—KAHLIL GIBRAN, twentieth-century Syrian-born mystic poet and philosopher

CONTENTS

PREFACE

Work is love made visible.

—KAHLIL GIBRAN

Y ou're not going to believe this, but my dad actually likes to work!" I recently overheard my ten-year-old daughter, Meryl Fé, say to a friend.

She's right. I love to work. Always have. I believe it provides a great sense of purpose and meaning, cultivates our capacity to serve, drives personal growth, stimulates creativity, and holds a key to collective evolution and transformation.

For the past three decades I have joyfully pursued my passion and calling: to discover and explore ways to become ever more human and fully present in the context of my work, to realize my highest potential to make the most substantial impact for the greatest good, and to support others in doing the same.

While this book is not an autobiography, it *is* personal because I developed the insights I share here through my own experience of working "for good." The Working for Good approach emerged as I cultivated the skills and practices I will describe and applied them in my own life. This approach has also been informed by my observation of and collaboration with others who have cultivated and applied some or all of these and related skills and practices.

I began writing the precursor to this book ten years ago, which I called *Building a Business with Soul*. My writing then, as now, was aimed at synthesizing the lessons I had learned with the unresolved questions and challenges I continued to explore. How do we build successful businesses that embody our highest aspirations and essential values? What practices increase the likelihood of creating sustainable conscious businesses? What factors undermine our ability to manifest our greatest intentions in business?

I've witnessed greed, fear, and delusion destroy relationships, waste resources, and undermine great potential for creating truly extraordinary, successful businesses. And I have witnessed success multiply when people transcend these forces.

Over the years, countless people have said to me, "You should write a book," generally after learning of my somewhat unusual journey and diverse experiences. Finally, one day I woke up and knew it was time to heed the call.

Writing this book has taken me deeper into the lessons I've learned and the skills I continue to hone, and it has profoundly validated the effectiveness of these skills. Practicing these skills supports us in pursuing our passion and our calling to serve the greatest good through our work. It also allows us to cultivate ourselves and each other in the process.

Business provides an incredible platform for expressing the full range of our humanity. At a historic Conscious Capitalism gathering in the fall of 2008, several of the presenters, including world-renowned management consultant Gary Hamel and Walter Robb, president and chief operating officer of Whole Foods Market, posed this question: "How do we build organizations that are as human as the people who inhabit them?" To this I add another question: How do *we* become more human in the context of our work, so we can build life-affirming organizations?

This book is about the life we choose to create for ourselves within our work, the businesses we bring to life, and how we relate to ourselves and each other in the process. I wrote most of it late at night after working full days. While I didn't intend or expect to do this, I soon realized that if I was going to write about Working for Good, I needed to be continually immersed in that process while I was writing, applying what I was writing about, and reflecting on it in the writing.

My principal work at this time is running a nonprofit organization called FLOW, dedicated to "liberating the entrepreneurial spirit for good." It was cofounded by John Mackey, CEO of Whole Foods Market, and Michael Strong, an educational entrepreneur committed to creating opportunity for all. John and Michael consider themselves to be libertarian do-gooders, committed to making the world a better place—convinced that entrepreneurship and markets are their most powerful tools. Michael is the "chief visionary officer" of FLOW. Drawing on substantial empirical evidence, he outlines the legal-system reforms and cultural shifts that foster entrepreneurial activity, and he tells inspiring stories of a world transformed for the better through the work of entrepreneurs who are motivated to do good.

I am FLOW's "chief activation officer." The title reflects my commitment to manifesting the FLOW vision and making real Michael's stories of healthy, thriving communities throughout the world and millions of people engaged in inspiring and meaningful work. As I told Michael and John when we began working together, I love ideas, but if they don't lead to action, I am not that interested.

In addition to general organizational and market development, a key element I bring to FLOW is the Cause Alliance Marketing model I have been developing for years. Cause Alliance Marketing programs catalyze multisector alliances to address social issues through integrated marketing campaigns, which simultaneously address the needs and objectives of program partners while leveraging their assets, resources, and capabilities in service to the cause, the alliance, and other partners. I am applying this model to FLOW outreach, education, and engagement programs called Peace Through Commerce, Accelerating Women Entrepreneurs, and Conscious Capitalism with the goals of increasing awareness of, attracting resources to, and facilitating participation in each of these emerging movements.

That's my day job. And during the day, as has been the case for many years, I collaborate with countless people. I often find myself facilitating meetings and supporting colleagues to be and do their best. Through this process, I have come to understand certain essential skills that foster the intention to work for the greater good and manifest goodness through work. This book is about these skills—what they are, how to develop them, and how to apply them in your work and your life.

Throughout my career, I have immersed myself in many idealistic ventures with great vision and high aspirations for serving humanity and making the world a better place. All of them have made meaningful contributions, and some continue to do so—and in some ways, all have fallen short of their aspirations.

This falling short inspires me to strive to fulfill a higher level of realization of the idea of Working for Good—and higher aspirations and steadfast pursuit generate great meaning and a powerful sense of purpose. When informed by the experience of repeatedly falling down, then successfully getting back up again—and by the world at first saying, "Are you crazy?" then beginning to say things like "This is a good idea" and "Let's see what we can do"—this aspiration and pursuit start to manifest a new, truly motivating reality.

HUMILITY

Perhaps the safest prediction we can make about the future is that it will surprise us.

—GEORGE LEONARD

The process of pursuing vision with passion and purpose is deeply humbling, as we fall short of our idealistic visions, see our personal shortcomings, are disappointed by others, and learn that things are not always what they seem to be.

There is a traditional Taoist story about a farmer. One day his only horse broke out of the corral and ran away. Upon hearing the news, the farmer's neighbors came to his house to see for themselves. They said, "Oh, what bad luck!" To which the farmer replied, "Maybe it is, maybe it isn't."

Within a week the horse returned, accompanied by a beautiful wild stallion, which the farmer and his son quickly corralled. Once again, upon hearing the news, the neighbors came to see for themselves. This time they proclaimed, "Oh, what good luck!" The farmer replied, "Maybe it is, maybe it isn't."

During his efforts to break the wild stallion, the farmer's son was thrown against a fence and broke his leg. True to form, the neighbors gathered round to console the farmer with "Oh, what bad luck!" And once again, the farmer replied, "Maybe it is, maybe it isn't."

At this time in China, two rival warlords were waging war against each other. The warlord over the Taoist farmer's village, who was one of the two combatants, visited the village to conscript young men to fight in the war. When his men came to take the farmer's son, they found him in pain and unable to walk, and left him behind while they gathered the rest of the young men in the village. Once again, the neighbors visited the farmer to congratulate him on his good fortune. And the farmer replied, "Maybe it is, maybe it isn't."

As this story represents, we never fully know the implications of anything, including our most well-intentioned efforts and apparent failures. Invariably and inevitably, we know less than we think we do. We can intend and aspire to serve the greatest good, and cultivate the skill to do so, but our sight and skill will always be limited, and there will always be others who see things differently. As my late grandmother used to say, "We don't see ourselves," and the aspects of ourselves we don't see can be the very things that limit our ability to manifest our visions or create conscious businesses. Here's one more story, to bring this point home:

When I was in my early twenties I commuted back and forth between Austin, Texas, and New York City, and I studied karate in both places. The teacher in Austin, Joe Alvarado, focused a lot on fighting and sparring. The school in New York, Mas Oyama's Kyokushin, emphasized form and drilling. Since I was doing both, I tended to be a bit quicker and sharper than my contemporaries in Austin, and a little more developed in sparring than my contemporaries in New York.

One day in New York, as part of a training session, I was invited to spar by Sensei Yoshi, a third-degree black belt and teacher from Japan I respected greatly. As I was apparently holding my own, he commented "good work."

The next moment, I found myself flat on the floor after he gently touched me on the top of my head with his foot— I didn't even see it happen.

The lesson in this has stayed with me for twenty-five years: be careful about what you think you know or are capable of, as there is likely to be someone more knowledgeable, experienced, and skillful right in front of you. So while passion, persistence, and even ferociousness will serve to advance our efforts to work for the greater good, openness, flexibility, and humility are essential.

My understanding of how to be human and bring my humanity into my work and business evolves all the time. As I spend more time with people like John Mackey, read the stories of others who run large companies, and share experiences with innumerable friends and colleagues who are entrepreneurs and change agents in business and in other contexts, I see more and more clearly that we are all engaged in exploration and discovery.

In *Working for Good*, I acknowledge a range of possibilities rather than a single road map to success. Conditions change, and people's perspectives, interpretations, and means of expression vary; there is no one right way. There is no magic solution, but there are ways to open to more magical, human experience and to be more skillful in facing the unknown and working with that constant and ultimately unpredictable force: change.

My intention with this book is to provide a meaningful context and the essential tools to support you in deeply and fully expressing your humanity through your work; to open to the vulnerability that makes you invulnerable; to establish a sense of aspirational purpose grounded in principles that sustain you in the face of adversity; and to find rich experience and deep fulfillment.

One of the most significant experiences I had when writing this book was slowing down, reflecting on my own experience and what I was observing in that of others, and allowing those lessons to inform an overall understanding and way of being. My primary orientation is to do and to move. My self-designated title of chief activation officer reflects my commitment and tendency to get things moving. And while this kind of kinetic energy is useful and even essential to moving things along, I find that the biggest breakthroughs and movements tend to happen in moments of stillness, when I stop *doing* and create space for *being*, within myself and others. As composer Claude Debussy once observed, "music is the space between the notes."

If you have ever meditated, gone through therapy, or taken part in other practices that slowed you down and provided opportunities to see and feel what was going on beneath the mind's chatter and the busyness of business, you understand the dynamic relationship between doing and being. You understand that you can consciously slow down and check in, then make choices about how to move from there. The simple acts of slowing down, checking in with yourself and others, and observing the conditions around you and the effects of your actions can start a whole series of events that can truly change the course of history.

For me, one of the greatest benefits of writing this book came when I sat down with more than a dozen friends and colleagues for extended conversations that focused on their work and their relationship to the idea of Working for Good. And my deepest satisfaction with the conversations was in hearing how much my friends and colleagues valued being listened to deeply and being able to express themselves in ways they had not done before. They became more connected to their own purpose and passion through our dialogue. To me, this is the essence and opportunity of Working for Good: showing up for each other, so we can more fully embody our potential, so we can co-create incredible manifestations of our highest intentions—for ourselves, for each other, and for all.

The other context in which I've refined my Working for Good skills is parenthood—specifically, being the father of a ten-year-old daughter. While it's not directly related to business, being a parent provides powerful lessons about presence, relationship, the connection between ideas and actions, and many other factors that are integral to being conscious in business. And my experience with parenthood also makes me especially sensitive to the needs of and constraints upon women entrepreneurs, working mothers, and other entrepreneurs who are single parents with young children.

I have learned that the line between work and life is one we manufacture. As Gandhi observed, "A man cannot do right in one department of life whilst he is occupied in doing wrong in any other department. Life is one invisible whole." Working for Good is principally about finding that wholeness in and through our work.

Chapter One

WHAT IS WORKING FOR GOOD?

*An individual has not started living until he can
rise above the narrow confines of his individualistic
concerns to the broad concerns of all humanity.*

—MARTIN LUTHER KING JR.

This book is about us—you and me and everyone else—and what we can do together to address the challenges and make the most of the opportunities facing humankind, to manifest a world that reflects our highest aspirations and most compelling visions.

In the opening of his classic book *Working*, Studs Terkel writes, "This book, being about work, is, by its very nature, about violence—to the spirit as well as to the body. It is about ulcers as well as accidents, about shouting matches as well as fistfights, about nervous breakdowns as well as kicking the dog around. It is, above all (or beneath all), about daily humiliations. To survive the day is triumph enough for the walking wounded among the great many of us."

This book, and the very idea of Working for Good, are meant to be an antidote to the violence people do to themselves and each other through business and work.

You may be reading this because you would like to do something to address some of the challenges facing humanity, because you believe that business provides an opportunity to do so, and because you want to understand more deeply how this vision can be manifested. This is what motivates many of us, especially young people; members of the Millennial Generation almost require that the companies they work for or build have a higher social purpose and act responsibly. You may also sense a calling to service and want to pursue it more fully. You may want to change your existing business or job, start a new business, or find a new place to work that is more deeply aligned with your purpose and principles. And you may want to learn new skills that will make you more effective in building a conscious business and make your business more responsive to the increasing market demand for good corporate citizenship. Working for Good acknowledges the power of these desires and provides tools for addressing them. It is a way of approaching work to serve the greater good.

Working for Good is a philosophy, a way of conducting business and approaching work that orients us on a path of personal growth, development, and service. Based in the skills and practices of awareness, embodiment, connection, collaboration, and integration, Working for Good guides our thoughts and actions to create businesses that value more than financial return on investment, respect people and the planet, deliver broad-based service to society, and promote widespread well-being.

By applying the skills of Working for Good, we bring out the best in ourselves and in others, increasing creativity, productivity, and sustainability. As measured by the Great Places to Work Institute, companies that treat employees as people, building trust and relationships, typically outperform their competitors and have lower absenteeism and workforce turnover. Happy employees have less stress and stress-related illness, and they cultivate happy customers—leading to sustained relationships and deeper loyalty. The virtuous cycle goes on. Companies that authentically serve the goals of Working for Good similarly engage sustained support from customers, employees, and their communities.

By Working for Good we find deeper meaning, make a greater impact through our work and, in the process, elevate each other and ourselves. Working for Good prepares us to adapt quickly, evolve continually, and respond skillfully to difficult people and challenging situations. And it opens us to opportunity and creativity. When we orient ourselves toward the Working for Good model and cultivate the five essential skills that are its focus, we can make a significant difference in our world. Perhaps the most difficult challenge of Working for Good is that of sustaining our faith—the faith that we *can* change the way people conduct business and conduct themselves in business. Each moment and in every situation, we have the choice to approach the people and situations we encounter, even the most challenging ones, with openness and compassion. And we can institutionalize the skills of Working for Good to cultivate a conscious culture within our business and between our business and the greater community. With sustained support from our internal and external communities, we can face ever-greater challenges while continuing to cultivate a more conscious way of conducting business.

The essence of Working for Good is a calling, a sense of passion and purpose that stirs us from deep inside and calls us to action. It is based on the belief that what we do matters, that we can make a difference—for ourselves, others, and the world—through the expression of our creativity and the application of our productive energy.

Working for Good is vital, invigorating, life-giving, meaning-making, fulfilling, and artful. It is also a strategy for success—for yourself, your colleagues, your business, and the broader community around you.

This book honors you for aspiring to Work for Good and for the Working for Good you are already engaged in. It is designed to inspire, validate, and deliver practical information. Choosing to Work for Good does not mean you are alone, crazy, or destined to poverty. On the contrary, you will begin to head toward a life full of meaning, joy, growth, and prosperity, in the fullest and deepest sense. In this book, you will be introduced to a larger vision of Working for Good, examples of the countless people successfully Working for Good, and practical tools to support you in your own pursuit of Working for Good.

The practical tools and exercises in this book are designed to cultivate the skills of Working for Good. The core of the book describes the five skills and their significance, presents exercises to cultivate them, and underscores the value of consistently practicing and employing them. With the book as your guide, you can proceed on your journey with confidence and energy.

WORKING FOR GOOD AND THE WORLD AT LARGE

We can't solve problems by using the same kind of thinking we used when we created them.

—ALBERT EINSTEIN

We live in a time of great change, significant challenges, and tremendous opportunity. Old ways of doing things don't work the way they once did, and we must continually experiment, adapt, and evolve. Globalization and the Internet exemplify an emerging new reality—or the recognition of a long-standing reality: we are all interconnected and interdependent. What happens in one place and to one person affects others and, in some way, affects us all. And in tangible and visible ways, issues like environmental contamination, financial system instability, HIV/AIDS propagation, water and food shortages, and political conflict clearly have global consequences. The world seems to be simultaneously more connected and more chaotic.

In this context, we ask ourselves, "What can I do?" "Who am I to make a difference in the face of such dramatic change on such an enormous scale?" "Where do I begin and how do I proceed?"

Human beings are the root of the problems we face, and of their solution. But, as Einstein suggests, to solve any problem we have to change the way we think and, thus, the way we act: from a me-centered worldview to one which is we-centered, which recognizes our interdependence; from short term to long term; from linear to holistic; from a perspective based on greed, fear, and delusion to one based on love, compassion, and trust.

Human beings have many extraordinary capabilities and capacities, and we can make a significant impact upon the world around us. Our challenges are to recognize and cultivate our talents and to apply them with purpose and passion, informed by deepening inquiry and awareness and refined and amplified through collaboration with others.

More than fifty years ago, pioneering psychologist Abraham Maslow introduced his "hierarchy of human needs," which represents a progression of human focus and orientation, from survival to transcendence, based on our material and social conditions and our cognitive, emotional, psychological, and spiritual development. Maslow observed that humans have certain universal needs. We need **physiological** sustenance: food, water, and air. We need **safety** from harm, including protection from the elements of nature (weather, fire, flood, etc.) and other people. We need **society**: relationships with others and a sense of belonging to a tribe or community. We need a sense of **self-esteem**: to be of value to others and to have a sense of self-worth. Finally, we are called to **self-actualization,** to fulfill our potential and, ultimately, to transcend our identification with an individual self and serve a higher purpose.

While people can feel fulfilled at any level to varying degrees, Maslow noted an almost universal pattern of progression through these stages. It seems that these needs build upon one another, with a person focusing on the more basic needs before progressing to the next level. In visual form, the hierarchy looks like Figure 1.

Maslow's model, which is congruent with many traditional spiritual systems, provided roots for the human potential movement that emerged in the 1960s and continues to evolve. New branches of this movement, validated through ongoing, rigorous research, recognize that we are complex and multi-dimensional beings, with multiple kinds of intelligence and

FIGURE 1

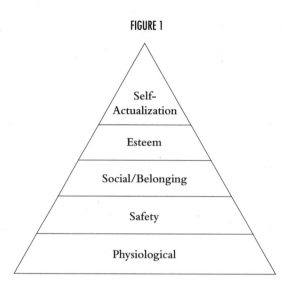

tremendous capacity for learning, growth, and development. They acknowledge that we can systematically become more consistently happy and fulfilled, and more present, creative, and effective. We have agency over our lives, and our lives can influence others and the world we co-create.

Driven in good part by the aging of the baby boomers, the largest generation in history, and fueled by the idealistic, impatient, action-oriented Millennials, we are witnessing a search for purpose and meaning on a massive scale and a reorientation of collective values from material to spiritual: we are now focusing on experience, beauty, and meaning rather than on things. The prominence of linear, rational, left-brain thinking is waning as that of holistic, intuitive, right-brain thinking waxes.

Arguably, there is a massive exodus, or elevation, from lower levels of Maslow's hierarchy to higher levels, and increasing recognition of the necessity and rewards of focusing on the greater good. Coincidentally, brain research indicates that doing good for others creates pleasure for the do-gooder on a biochemical level, and psychological research substantiates the common-sense notion that serving others creates a sense of purpose and increases happiness.

As our work at FLOW reflects, a growing transpartisan or nonpartisan movement is emerging, with similar reflections in many fields. Philosophers like Ken Wilber maintain that we are witnessing the emergence of significant numbers of people who embody a new level of integral consciousness focusing on what unites rather than separates, what adds to a greater whole rather than "my idea versus yours," and what elevates us all rather than what puts me ahead of you. We are celebrating unity in diversity, the individual and the interdependent whole.

Our recognition of interdependence, quest for meaning, and drive to do good are all influencing business. For more than a decade, consumer polls have indicated that people expect companies to provide more to the community than merely selling products and services, and they reward companies that are good citizens. A new model for business is emerging in which entrepreneurs and corporate leaders acknowledge interdependence and bring it to the forefront, catalyzing systems of interrelated stakeholder groups—customers, team members, investors, vendors, the community—connected by shared purpose and cultivated through thoughtful consideration and engagement.

Stories of new ways of doing business appear in countless books and studies—by researchers, entrepreneurs, and successful CEOs—addressing the topics of authentic leadership, relationship marketing, workforce empowerment, and similar themes, celebrating the power of nonmaterial and nonrational factors. Purpose and relationship have become driving forces in fueling business success, in even the largest of companies. For example, John Mackey tells of meeting with Indra Nooyi, CEO of PepsiCo, and her goal of leading Pepsi to become a "good company."

The healthy functioning of the market process is driving much of the transformation of business as we collectively recognize the need to consider the effects of our activities on the environment and each other, and as we demand that businesses address them as part of their service.

OPPORTUNITIES ABOUND

> *People must be motivated by a deeper cause. I believe that people don't come to work to earn money for themselves and the company. They come to work because the product does something worthwhile, and this is what gets people inspired.*
>
> —BILL GEORGE

The dramatic circumstances of our times, an emerging new reality, and increasing new demands provide profound opportunities for business. And while business as an institution is often criticized and even demonized, business is a powerful force for positive change. Its processes and products captivate our attention and energy, influence our consciousness, and affect our material, psychological, and spiritual well-being.

Through business, entrepreneurs catalyze the convergence of ideas, energy, and resources to create new products and services, develop new technologies, solve problems, capitalize on opportunities, stretch our imaginations, and increase our concept of what is possible.

Business is not a mechanical system that exists separately from humanity, but a way of organizing our collective productive activity that reflects our view of nature and the world and our needs, desires, and expectations. It exists within the context of the natural, physical world and our perceptions and expectations. And as the world and our perceptions change, so too does this context.

We increasingly recognize interdependencies and the effect business has—on the environment, society, and individual people—when it is viewed and operated as a mechanistic, independent process that is not responsible to the communities and environment that form its context. And we are revisioning and redefining why businesses exist, what they do, and how they do it. As entrepreneurs, investors, employees, consumers, or citizens, we *are* business. Since we conceive it, manage and staff it, legislate it, and buy its products and services, we influence what business is and what it does.

While the popular view has traditionally been that "the business of business is business," a new concept is emerging that balances the pursuit of profit with service to life: human beings and their communities, present and future, and the natural world.

We require that what we do and how we do it through business have more depth and meaning. The way we communicate and work together can be clearer and more collaborative, creative, and productive. Our decisions can be more considerate of our customers, our employees, our community, and the environment. We observe that the world and how we think about it are changing, and we see the possibility—in fact, the necessity—for the way we view and do business to change as well.

The emerging new role for business is one of responsible citizenship and direct engagement in addressing the challenges and opportunities humanity faces.

CONSCIOUS BUSINESS AND CONSCIOUS CAPITALISM

In a healthy, complex, evolving, and self-adapting system the harmony of interests between stakeholders proves to be far more important and resilient than the various conflicts of interest that the analytic mind focuses upon.

—JOHN MACKEY

The Conscious Business model that John Mackey and FLOW promote offers an encouraging and inspiring new perspective on business. Conscious Business rests on three core principles. The first is that every business has the opportunity to create and embody a deeper purpose beyond return on shareholder investment. That purpose can be anything as long as it inspires those who carry it and delivers service to others. The second principle of Conscious Business is that every business exists within a system of interrelated and interdependent stakeholders, and the best way to manage a business is to optimize the interdependent system, serving and creating value for all stakeholders— customers, employees, investors, suppliers, community, and the environment. The third principle is that of servant leadership, which reflects an orientation of service for leaders throughout the business, beginning with the CEO. Research indicates—and John's experience with Whole Foods Market suggests—that companies embracing this model create the greatest long-term value for investors. The Whole Foods Market "Declaration of Interdependence" explicitly states the company's purpose—to serve people and planet—and acknowledges the company's relationship to its stakeholders, including employees, customers, and the planet. It sets forth the company's mission to serve and engage its stakeholders in a co-creative relationship.

The emerging Conscious Business movement has many faces, pioneers, and even heroes who recognize the power of purpose, the centrality of interdependence, and the role of service. John Mackey, Walter Robb (President and COO of Whole Foods Market), and their executive team have built an interdependent stakeholder model and a dynamic, world-class team member empowerment structure and culture, which is essential to the success of Whole Foods Market.

Jim Sinigal, CEO of Costco, receives great flak from Wall Street for taking a salary below $500,000 while his multibillion dollar company continues to grow. Costco also operates with a powerful empowerment culture, paying its team members substantially more than competitor Wal-Mart while providing them with substantial benefits.

Chip Conley, CEO of Joie de Vivre Hospitality, a chain of boutique hotels on the West Coast, and author of *Peak: How Great Companies Get Their Mojo from Maslow*, has similarly established a culture designed to support the growth and development of his team members. Joie de Vivre's salaried employees receive a month paid sabbatical for every three years of continuous employment. During the cataclysmic market collapse in 2001, Chip and JDV sustained this policy and deepened their commitment to team member empowerment and stakeholder elevation, with profoundly positive results.

Ray Anderson, CEO of Interface Carpets, is renowned for his pioneering approach to environmental sustainability, transforming his multibillion dollar company from a seller of disposable, toxic carpeting to one that rents environmentally sustainable, recyclable carpeting on a mass scale—based on the cradle-to-cradle model, popularized by Bill McDonough and Michael Braungart, in which materials from products are reused or recycled to create new products, rather than becoming waste.

Sally Jewel, CEO of REI (the sporting goods retailer) and Terri Kelly, CEO of W. L. Gore & Associates (makers of cutting-edge synthetics including Gore-Tex, and many of the products made from them) lead their respective companies in the pioneering tradition in which each was founded, setting an inspiring example to other aspiring Conscious Capitalists.

The aggregated corps of Conscious Businesses and Conscious Capitalists form an emerging Conscious Capitalism movement. And the lead actors on the stage of Conscious Capitalism are not limited to business entrepreneurs and corporate leaders. The 2006 Nobel Peace Laureate Muhammad Yunus, and the for-profit Grameen Bank he founded, have established a new model for banking, opening opportunities for the poorest of the poor—mainly women and their families—with innovative, collateral-free loans. Bill Drayton of Ashoka and others like him have catalyzed a flourishing Social Entrepreneurship movement, with legions of social entrepreneurs applying the processes of business to social service and fostering innovation, empowerment, and scalable change.

The marketplace of innovation around business structure itself is robust. Dr. Yunus advocates what he calls Social Business. These are businesses that have a social mission at their core; while they function as for-profit companies, investors see a limited return on their investment, recouping it but accruing no interest or appreciation. This model creates a purposeful hybrid of investment and philanthropy, fostering organizations that function effectively in the competitive marketplace for social change to return their investors' capital, but that are not driven to generate huge profits or dividends. As a result, their resources can be focused on the social mission.

Terry Mollner, president of the Trusteeship Institute and a founder of the Calvert Social Investment Funds and Shareholders Capital, Inc., celebrates "common good corporations," which are comfortable breaking even and even losing money—as long as the common good is being served in the expectation that in the long term they will be more profitable than their competitors using this business ethic.

Pennsylvania-based B Lab cofounders Jay Coen Gilbert, Bart Houlahan, and Andrew Kassoy have created a certification system for B Corporations, which explicitly use the power of business to create public benefit. B Corporations must "meet comprehensive and transparent social and environmental performance standards; legally expand the responsibilities of the corporation to include stakeholder interests; and build collective voice through the power of the unifying B Corporation brand."

This movement to transform business is reflected in the attention and actions of investors. Building on the steady growth of the social investment sector, which began with social screens for investments in conventional companies, a new investment sector is emerging to support and leverage Conscious Capitalism and other forms of social businesses. Yogi Bhajan, the late spiritual teacher, used to say, "Money is what money does," and money is increasingly aligning with the emerging Conscious

Capitalism and Social Business movement. This includes venture capital firms focused on companies with multiple bottom lines, community banks like New Resource Bank in San Francisco, which targets its loans to companies with environmentally sustainable products and services, and ShoreBank in Chicago, which focuses on local community development.

Countless entrepreneurs in diverse industries are staking out new paths to creating conscious companies in service to the greater good.

Through his Volcano Island Honey company, Richard Spiegel produces some of the best honey in the world using the most labor-intensive and environmentally sensitive practices, supports the personal growth of his local team members, and provides deep discounts to local community members so they can afford to purchase his very expensive, exclusive, gourmet honey.

Traci Fenton's WorldBlu promotes the practice of organizational democracy through educational services, an annual list called the WorldBlu List of Most Democratic Workplaces™, and conferences and other events. Traci's work facilitates and celebrates democratically designed organizations.

Zak Zaidman of Kopali Organics is supporting family farmers and protecting important ecosystems in Costa Rica and other places where Kopali sources its products, delivering the highest-quality organic snacks while paying fair prices to farmers. Through these premium products, Zak is helping to "restore a healthy connection between the food we eat, the lives of the farmers who grow it, and the planet we all share."

Colombian-born Marcella Echavarria's mission is to elevate the people and cultures of the southern hemisphere, to create a sense of self-respect and pride, and to catalyze healthy economies derived from the beauty emerging from their cultures and the skills of the people. Through SURevolution, Marcella delivers the highest-quality artisan products to the luxury market in New York and other major cities, paying good wages and providing training and other services to the artisans.

Like Marcella, Senegalese entrepreneur Magatte Wade is passionately committed to elevating the stature and conditions of Africa and Africans. Several years ago, when she returned to her native Senegal after years away, she noted that the traditional hibiscus-based beverage was scarcely seen, giving way to popular global sodas. Distraught, she started Adina World Beat Beverages, beginning with hibiscus-based Senegalese bissap, intent on making it popular in the United States so that it would again be "cool" to drink in Senegal. After a successful start-up and transition to seasoned managers, Magatte is on to her next ventures to elevate the conditions of and increase opportunities for Senegalese and other African women so they can become entrepreneurs in the world market.

Cheryl Fields Tyler's Blue Beyond Consulting provides world-class business strategy and change management consulting services to multinational corporations and nonprofits. Her purpose is to help her clients improve organizational performance in ways that both deliver bottom-line value and enhance people's lives. And her company is commited to being a generative source for good.

Stories like these abound and new ones emerge every day, as entrepreneurs and social entrepreneurs dedicated to service heed the call and venture into the great adventure of creating conscious businesses.

Emerging new collective understanding and yearnings—along with increasing demand from consumers, employees, investors, and communities that business serve higher needs and conduct itself responsibly—create tremendous opportunities for companies to become more conscious, connected, and integrated. This new context provides opportunities for new products and services, as well as new ways of conducting business.

ENTREPRENEURS OF MEANING

Business is a creative and therefore spiritual endeavor. Great entrepreneurs enter the field of business in the same way great artists enter the field of art. With their business creation, entrepreneurs express their spiritual desire for self-realization, evolutionary passion for self-fulfillment, and creative vision of a new world. The entrepreneur's business is their artwork. The creation of business is as creative as any creation in art. In fact, building a business may be the most creative human activity.

—YASUHIKO KIMURA

Entrepreneurs are artists who like to get things done and make things happen. They tend to be passionate, driven, impatient, and even impetuous. They solve problems and capitalize on opportunities. Through their ideas, inventions, creations, and endeavors, entrepreneurs change the way we think and live.

To some extent, we are all entrepreneurs, as we focus our creativity and productive energy to address challenges and pursue opportunities. On the most basic level, we are all entrepreneurs of survival. It is built into our DNA. Most of us apply our creativity and productive energy through our work, whether we start businesses, manage them, or work in them. As our entrepreneurial DNA is fully activated, we continuously look for more and bigger problems to solve and opportunities to capitalize on.

If they are to catalyze a business system around their ideas, all entrepreneurs have to generate meaning for themselves and others. To create a transformational, conscious business, an entrepreneur has to tap into higher aspirations and conduct business in ways that align with them.

While not exclusively focused on entrepreneurs, this book acknowledges and celebrates the generative role they play in addressing challenges, leveraging opportunities, driving change, creating value, and catalyzing meaning.

Increasing numbers of entrepreneurs are focusing directly on the greatest challenges facing humankind, including environmental degradation, health crises, poverty, political conflict, and the quest for meaning. The innovative and generative energy of entrepreneurs and entrepreneurship is essential to addressing these issues.

And developing new forms of business and investment structures and practices is an entrepreneurial activity in itself. We can apply the skills and energy of entrepreneurship—which include innovation, risk-taking, animating a vision, and catalyzing resources—to create something new, to transform the way we conduct business.

THE WORKING FOR GOOD APPROACH: THE PROCESS IS THE PRODUCT

Mind is the forerunner of all things.

—THE BUDDHA

Ideas are powerful. Varied perspectives, mind-sets, and orientations manifest different actions, which create distinct effects. Our actions reflect our beliefs and thought patterns, which create and transform our world.

If we believe the world is a dangerous jungle where everyone and everything is out to get us, we will behave one way. If we believe that the universe is organized by a great God, everything is predetermined in an orderly pattern, and our job is to play our clearly scripted part in the story, we will act in another way. And if we believe we are experiencing the emergence of an age of transcendence, and that we are expressing and participating in its evolution, we will work in still other ways.

Working for Good is based on the understanding that mind is the origin of our reality. Our thoughts drive our actions, which manifest our reality. We create what we envision, whether it is a toaster oven, Las Vegas, or a man landing on the moon. All of these began with an idea. India's independence from Britain was attained through Gandhi's vision of a revolution based on nonviolent resistance. The examples, small and large, of the power of mind are endless.

Fortunately, our sense of what is important, our scope of identification, and our relationship to ideas are all open to development, refinement, and expansion based on our ideas—as are our behaviors and actions. The search for meaning and purpose, the aspiration to self-actualization and transcendence, and the recognition of interdependence provide tremendous opportunity to envision and cultivate new ways of organizing and conducting business. They call for us to show up with all our human capacity and purposefully cultivate skills for being more fully human, so we can work within a web of cooperative relationships and effectively respond to rapidly changing circumstances.

As entrepreneurs, managers, team members, investors, and other actors in business, we continually deal with uncertainty, challenges, conflicts, overload, and their related stress. How we deal with them is key to our success and well-being.

The Working for Good approach recognizes that our businesses are expressions of our humanity and platforms for cultivating what it means to be human. Through business we address the full range of our needs, from survival to transcendence. In this context, we can systematically apply the skills and practices of awareness, embodiment, connection, collaboration, and integration to develop discernment, deepen relationships, enhance performance, cultivate presence, and sustain the passionate pursuit of purpose.

The Working for Good approach recognizes that knowing our purpose is critical and knowing ourselves is essential. It calls for us to observe and understand what we think and feel, and how our thoughts and feelings affect our perspectives, attitudes, relationships, and performance. It asks us to look deeply at our intentions and actions and how they affect outcomes. And it asks us to know the principles and values that guide our actions, as they reflect what we stand for, and what we will take a stand for.

In Working for Good, the product of our work is intimately connected to the process by which we work. What we create through our businesses reflects the way we conduct ourselves in business. In many ways, the process is the product.

Above all, the Working for Good approach supports us in cultivating specific skills that enable us to make conscious choices and embody those choices through conscious action—and, as a result, manifest conscious businesses. Working for Good illuminates and celebrates the opportunity we have to create productive, sustainable businesses, happy,

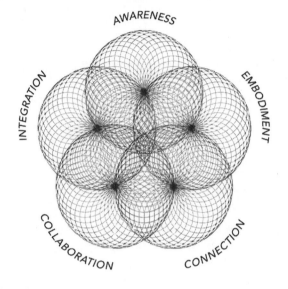

healthy people, and a sane and humane world, based on the choices we make and the way we embody our choices.

The Essential Skills of Working for Good

The Essential Skills of Working for Good are:

- Awareness
- Embodiment
- Connection
- Collaboration
- Integration

The combination of these five skills forms an integrated Working for Good system. While each skill is connected to and informs the others, there is a progression of development and application from awareness to embodiment, connection, collaboration, and integration.

Awareness is the mother of all skills. It is our foundation as human beings. In any given moment or circumstance, awareness enables us to sense and consider our internal and external environment, state of being, mind-set, and relationship to the world around us. Through awareness, we can recognize the effect of circumstances and events, the effect we have on others, and the effect others have on us.

Awareness asks questions that seek to penetrate, to get behind facades and into the depths. What's going on here? How can we move with it or transform it? Awareness begins with and within ourselves and moves outward from there. Our connection to purpose and guiding principles emerges from the ground, the base, of awareness.

Awareness is essential, but if it isn't embodied in actions, its effects are minimized. So a key step in activating awareness is embodiment. If we are to be truly conscious, awareness needs to be embodied—literally carried in our bodies—and manifested through our actions and behaviors. Embodiment means moving from awareness into action; it is the place where we "walk our talk" and otherwise act in alignment with our intentions.

Connection begins with cultivating awareness—connecting with ourselves and working with our minds and hearts—and emerges as we carry awareness into embodiment, into action with our bodies. From here we connect with others, building bridges of shared understanding and aligned action. On the most basic level, we connect by recognizing a shared interest. More deeply, though, we connect by recognizing and respecting each other's humanity. And we foster even deeper connection by loosening our hold on our ideas and beliefs and opening to those of others. We let go of our attempts to control or manipulate and enter into the possibility of co-creation.

This letting go opens us to the realm of what a college professor of mine called "creative chaos," the place where deep connection, authentic relationship, and profound insight are born. Here, the hard walls of our egos soften to allow us to open to other ways of seeing and being. Coming from embodied awareness, we have firm ground to stand upon and purposeful direction, so our openness creates not confusion but opportunity.

Connection opens the way to true collaboration: explicit, purposeful co-creation, working together to manifest something that we envision together in a way that reflects the ongoing cultivation of embodied awareness. As with any of the essential skills, we can cultivate collaboration through practice, learning and applying time-tested techniques and methods to facilitate it. But techniques and methods alone do not facilitate deep, sustained collaboration. To be most effective, we need to apply them with awareness and genuine openness to connection, lest they become rigid, mechanical, and manipulative.

Collaboration leads to integration and completes the full circle of the Working for Good system. Integration is the dynamic process of combining various elements into a new whole that has its own presence and integrity. As we cultivate and embody awareness and connect and collaborate with others, we become something more than we were before. This, in turn, informs our awareness and our ability to embody, connect, and collaborate, creating a virtuous cycle of learning, growth, and development.

Integration fosters recognition of interdependence and openness to all that exists, and it requires skillful means of coming to terms with what disturbs us and what we might otherwise resist, including blind spots, shadows, conflict, and dissident voices.

Working for Good is an emergent process of unfolding awareness. Conditions change. Old approaches no longer work. Our awareness evolves. The way we co-create with others changes. We bring our new awareness into the world through our work, and the cycle continues.

WHAT IS DIFFERENT ABOUT WORKING FOR GOOD AND WHAT ARE ITS BENEFITS?

> *Knowing others is intelligence;*
> *knowing yourself is true wisdom.*
> *Mastering others is strength;*
> *mastering yourself is true power.*
>
> —LAO TZU, *Tao Te Ching*

Most people work for good in one way or another—creating value, providing for their families, and generating meaning and community for themselves and others. And countless companies are bringing great things into the world through useful products and services, the jobs and wealth they create, and the contributions they make to their communities and the world through philanthropy and service—beyond what they deliver through their core business.

As I have described, many new approaches to organizing and conducting business are emerging, including Conscious

Business, Social Business, B Corporations, and "common good corporations." Rather than a system of organizing a company's structure, Working for Good is a way of showing up for work, regardless of the organization's structure or the products and services it produces.

In companies oriented toward profit over all else, with no regard for people or planet, the environment is often one of rampant fear, greed, delusion, and a numbing of the human spirit. People are treated as a means rather than an end, without regard for their health or well-being. High stress leads to illness and reduced productivity. Rather than operating as a united front pursuing a common goal, the attitude is one of "everyone for themselves."

In many respects, Working for Good is the antidote to this kind of working environment. It can even be considered a spiritual practice. We commit to embodying and cultivating the practice of the five essential skills, even while facing the daily exigencies of work and building our businesses. Then we reinvest the fruits of the practice directly back into our work.

By systematically cultivating and applying the skills of Working for Good, we become more aware of how we are showing up to work, our effect on others, and their effect on us. We recognize the stories we tell ourselves and how they influence and inform our actions. We become less identified with our egos and roles, more easily admit and learn from our mistakes, and adjust our perspective and course of action accordingly.

By loosening the grip of embedded conditioning and mental programs, we can more deeply connect with our purpose, passion, and principles and embody them with greater ease and more energy. We become more flexible, less interested in control, and more open to dispersed responsibility and deeper collaboration.

Applying the skills of Working for Good has profound benefits for our work and our lives in general. Since they are the skills of cultivating our humanity, they elevate our level of functioning and enhance our ability to connect, collaborate, and integrate. Let's look at the full circle of essential skills again and what each contributes:

- Awareness leads to insight, creativity, sensitivity, responsiveness, and skillfulness in managing ourselves and working with others.
- Embodiment builds congruity, authenticity, dependability, trust, and powerful presence, which attracts and engages others.
- Connection fosters sensitivity to issues and opportunities, facilitates shared learning, builds relationships, and leads to collaboration.
- Collaboration fosters synergies, generates new ideas and opportunities, and releases productive energy.
- Integration releases blocks, resolves conflicts, incorporates new understandings, increases integrity and sustainability, amplifies presence, and leads to new levels of awareness and performance.

Applying these skills in an ongoing, systematic way cultivates a conscious system with deep, authentic relationships. It feeds hope, optimism, and confidence, and cultivates loyalty relationships between a business's various stakeholders.

Because Working for Good skills support our personal and collective growth and development and cultivate higher levels of identification and service, over time the products, services, and businesses we create become more conscious and focused on serving the greater good.

Noted psychologist and Holocaust survivor Viktor Frankl advised, "Don't aim at success—the more you aim at it and make it a target, the more you are going to miss it. For success, like happiness, cannot be pursued; it must ensue, and it only does so as the unintended side effect of one's personal dedication to a cause greater than oneself or as the by-product of one's surrender to a person other than oneself."

In his definition of Conscious Business, John Mackey suggests that the higher purpose of a business is whatever is essential to the business that inspires and motivates the entrepreneurs and other stakeholders. It does not need to be specifically focused on the greater good, as long as the purpose is true for the people involved in the business.

The purpose of a business can evolve over time as it becomes more complex, as the environment changes, and as interactions between the stakeholders and the business shape it. In the emerging new context, customers, employees, communities, and other stakeholders are demanding that companies serve the greater good; more entrepreneurs are starting businesses focused on serving the greater good; and more executives are exploring how to shift the focus of large corporations more towards the greater good.

As Robb Smith, CEO of Integral Life, observes, "My purpose when I was twenty-one was a lot different from what it is now. Then, I was focused on making money and making my mark. Now, as a father, and having achieved material success, I am more focused on meaning and service, being a good parent, and creating a world that is healthy and safe for my son."

The skills of Working for Good facilitate and accelerate this evolution of awareness and purpose and its reflection through our actions. As a result, we end up creating businesses that more directly serve the greater good, both through what they produce and how they do so.

The challenges facing humanity are clear opportunities for business. The marketplace is saying "yes!" to environmental sustainability, poverty alleviation, peace, and opportunity for all—and business is responding. Consumers, employees, investors, and others expect businesses to participate in addressing social issues, and they look to business as a source of inspiration, meaning, and purpose as well as a platform for personal growth and societal evolution.

Working for Good companies will more fully realize the potential of business to serve as a positive agent for change. They create a healthy, sustainable model for business in service to society, based on strong, resilient relationships. And they advance the evolution of the marketplace as a tool to facilitate human interaction and development.

While some may question the practicality of Working for Good, I maintain that, from a personal, professional, and societal perspective, there is nothing more practical we can do; it fosters creativity, resilience, energy, and community, leading to broad-based and sustainable success.

If this book and the ideas behind Working for Good are to be practical for you, they will need to teach you to derive many of the benefits I have outlined, including increasing the sustainable success of your business, your ability to stay grounded and centered in the face of change, and your sense of ease, well-being, and peace of mind. I intend to do all I can to deliver these and other benefits. In the chapters ahead, we will begin our work together to manifest this intention.

PUTTING WORKING FOR GOOD INTO PRACTICE

An ounce of practice is worth a ton of theory.
　　　　　　　　　　　　—ANONYMOUS TAOIST MASTER

Practice is at the heart of Working for Good. As is true of all accomplishments and skills, becoming a conscious entrepreneur and change agent at work and building a successful conscious business require diligent practice: the ongoing, systematic repetition of specific exercises to cultivate proficiency, skill, and, ideally, mastery. While we attend to the daily demands and requirements of building our businesses, practice ensures that we cultivate what is essential to us and finely hone skills to draw upon during intense and challenging times.

You may have heard the story of the man who goes into the forest every day to cut trees, but doesn't sharpen his axe. A passerby, observing that he is making little progress in his efforts, asks him why he doesn't sharpen his axe. He responds, "I don't have time. I've got too many trees to cut down." When I lived in Mexico, I spent a lot of time with a master gardener named Hugo, who could do more work, with apparently less effort, than several "normal" people. Before he started his work for the day, he would frequently sit for an extended time, slowly and carefully filing the edge of his hoe. He knew that a sharp hoe would do the work his arms wouldn't have to do. Similarly, Don Nacho, the nearly eighty-year-old *palmero* who climbed forty-foot-high palm trees to cut their leaves, would sit patiently sharpening his machete, checking the edge from time to time until it was just right. Then he would ascend to the heights and cut with ease.

Sharpening our tools is both literal and metaphorical. We can apply Hugo's and Don Nacho's approach of slowing down, checking, and sharpening to our tools of awareness, embodiment, connection, collaboration, and integration.

Part of practice is learning from our mistakes, since we can learn as much from those as from our successes. Basketball immortal Michael Jordan said about himself, "I've missed more than nine thousand shots in my career. I've lost almost three hundred games. Twenty-six times I've been trusted to take the game-winning shot and missed. I've failed over and over and over again in my life. And that is why I succeed."

When asked what the key to success is, billionaire serial entrepreneur Sam Wyly quickly replies, "perseverance." A line in the refrain from one of my favorite songs goes, "It's not the falling down that matters, it's the getting up again." This spirit of persistence and relentless pursuit is essential to manifesting Working for Good, as it is to any worthwhile endeavor.

Psychologist Martin Seligman, leader of the Positive Psychology movement, notes that the key to perseverance is optimism—and this is an orientation we can cultivate and learn. The key to cultivating optimism is self-awareness.

In the next five chapters, I will present various practices for each of the essential skills of Working for Good. They draw on decades of direct experience that led toward Working for Good—both mine and that of colleagues and collaborators who share a similar purpose and passion.

In Chapter Two, "Awareness," we will start with a progression of practices related to Awareness of Self, Awareness in Relationship to Others, and Awareness in Relationship to Groups. In Chapter Three, "Embodiment," we will focus on how to carry awareness into action. Chapter Four, "Connection," addresses how we bring embodied awareness into relationships and lay the groundwork for collaboration. In Chapter Five, "Collaboration," we will focus on how we move from ideas to action with others. Then in Chapter Six, "Integration," we will tie all of these together and address other issues relevant to creating an integrated system of Working for Good.

In the spirit of my role as chief activation officer, I will do my best to make these skills easy to understand and apply, and I will work to cultivate an experience of their interconnectedness.

WORKING FOR GOOD MATTERS

I know of no more encouraging fact than the unquestionable ability of man to elevate his life by conscious endeavor.
—HENRY DAVID THOREAU

What we think and do matters. What we envision, we can manifest. By cultivating the skills of Working for Good, we can make a profound difference for ourselves, for others, and for the world.

Human beings have conceived and built the pyramids and the Taj Mahal, have sent probes to Mars and seen inside atoms, ended apartheid in South Africa, and eradicated countless plagues. And, yes, we also continue to create and uncover new challenges and manifest both our generative and destructive capacities.

Just as countless individuals and organizations are choosing to do, we too can apply our creative, productive energy through our work and businesses to address these challenges, mitigate our own destructive activity, and serve ourselves, our families, our communities, our species, and all life on Earth. Through our entrepreneurial initiative and the way we conduct business, we can directly address pressing social issues, advance human evolution, and establish new ways of being human that help all involved to flourish. That is Working for Good!

> *It takes creative individuals with fixed determination and indomitable will to propel the innovation that society needs to tackle its toughest problems. It shows that an important social change frequently begins with a single entrepreneurial author: one obsessive individual who sees a problem and envisions a new solution, who takes the initiative to act on that vision, who gathers resources and builds organizations to protect and market that vision, who provides that energy and sustained focus to overcome the inevitable resistance, and who—decade after decade—keeps improving, strengthening, and broadening that vision until what was once a marginal idea has become a new norm.*
>
> —DAVID BORNSTEIN, *How to Change the World*

Reflection on Writing

Writing is a powerful tool for reflection and self-expression. At the end of each month I write two monthly newsletters entitled *Reflections* and *FLOW Action News,* which disciplines me to reflect systematically on the preceding month: to acknowledge key developments, to recognize lingering challenges, to discern lessons learned, and to express them in a way that makes sense to others. Reflection supports the development of awareness, embodiment, connection, collaboration, and integration.

Writing provides the feedback loop, holding up a mirror to our thoughts. Journaling, emailing, letter-writing, and even texting give us the opportunity to reflect on our experiences, integrate them for ourselves, and convey our perceptions to others.

At the end of each chapter ahead I will encourage you to take time to reflect and write what emerges. You can direct your writing toward yourself, others, or both. As you work on many of the exercises in this book, you may also want to take time to record your thoughts.

Writing reflections is an activity you can carry with you everywhere you go. While I used to be teased for taking notes all the time, I am thankful now that I cultivated the process of taking notes and reflecting on my experiences. My writing not only provided material for this book and my work in general, but the process exercises my capacity for inquiry, investigation, reflection, self-expression, and communication.

A Note on the Exercises in This Book

You will find exercises interspersed throughout the chapters that follow. They are designed to support you in cultivating the skills of Working for Good.

You can approach these exercises in several ways. First, you can practice the exercises as you are reading them, or you can read through them first and then practice them. If you prefer to hear them read out loud, you can visit workingforgood.com/exercises to find each exercise in audio format. Hearing the practices aloud will allow you to close your eyes while you practice, which is helpful for many of the exercises.

Chapter Two

AWARENESS

He who cannot change the very fabric of his thought will
never be able to change reality, and will never,
therefore, make any progress.

—ANWAR SADAT

M arcella Echavarria, the entrepreneur behind
SURevolution, has always been empathic—especially at work. In the past, her problem was that
she mirrored the emotional state of her colleagues. When
someone in her working life was having a bad day—if they
were sick, in a bad mood, or otherwise in a negative or
unhealthy state—Marcella, too, would have a bad day. She
found herself suddenly feeling under the weather, in a foul
mood, or sitting in judgment of those around her. At the
time, however, she didn't even realize what was happening.

Then Marcella began practicing yoga and meditation.
Through ongoing practice, she developed an expanded
awareness. She began to see how she mirrored the emotional

states of those around her, and was able to develop a sense of perspective and non-identification, balanced by care and compassion. Now, when someone is sick or in a bad mood or is aggravating in some way, she recognizes that it is not about her—and she can separate from their experience. She will go so far as to call the person sitting at a desk right next to her on the phone rather than talk with them directly if she knows that the conversation will go better on the phone than face to face. At the same time, without getting entangled in or identified with the other person's emotions, Marcella empathizes and sends them good wishes. She finds that this approach reduces dramatic encounters and even gives the other person the opportunity to turn their own mind state around.

....

Awareness: Knowledge or perception of a state, situation, or fact, drawn from and focused on internal or external experience. Conscious or self-awareness is the condition of being aware of our awareness, to guide our behavior.

....

Awareness is a catalyst for changing the fabric of our own thought, facilitating growth, and working with others. It gives birth to the other four skills of Working for Good and forms the ground of our being—the membrane connecting who we are, who others are, and the reality we co-create.

Like love, compassion, and empathy, awareness is a meta-skill, or a skill that enhances the way we apply other skills. When we communicate with awareness or love, we are more effective than when we do so without them. Awareness makes us human and enables us to ascend to higher levels of self-actualization, service, and self-transcendence. It also activates the process of Working for Good, fostering embodiment, connection, collaboration, and integration.

As we move into this exploration of awareness, we'll start with a few assumptions, including some we have already visited.

- *Much more is unknown to us than is known.* Reality is a vast ocean, and we understand the nature and functioning of only a few grains of sand on the beach.
- *Who we are is relative.* It changes based on our circumstances, our personal evolution, and the relationship between the two.
- *We co-create one another and the world.* We are individual reflections of a greater whole, and the whole reflects who we are. We create the world and the world creates us.
- *What we do matters.* Whatever reality actually is, we can experience—alone and with one another—the good, the true, the beautiful, and the divine, however we perceive them. While we may have different interpretations of our experience, to the extent that we form groups with shared understandings, what we do matters to what we experience, how we exist, and what we co-create. Because we can know, for ourselves and with others, that there are such experiences as the good, true, and beautiful, we can embody and manifest them, and we can change the world to reflect and cultivate these experiences.

The late philosopher Alan Watts powerfully conveyed the relative nature of reality—and the essential role that we play in creating reality and that the world plays in creating us—in his reflection on rainbows. I will paraphrase it here:

Consider a rainbow. For a rainbow to exist, three factors come into play: sunlight, moisture in the air, and the eyes to perceive it, all perfectly aligned. Without any one of these factors, there is no rainbow. If you have ever chased a rainbow, you know that you can't catch it. It moves as we move and as the relationships between the sun, the moisture, and our eyes change. We can only see a rainbow or have the experience of it if there are sun and moisture. Our reality is informed, if not defined, by the world around us.

A Moment of Awareness and a Story

As we enter more deeply into awareness and prepare to work with specific practices to cultivate awareness, I want to acknowledge something and, in the process, model the practice of awareness. In this and other chapters you will see stories and anecdotes from Buddhist and other spiritual traditions. I include them here because, given their focus on cultivating awareness, these traditions are rich with great, illustrative tales.

The practice I am modeling in this passage is making explicit what might otherwise not be, thus raising our awareness of what I am doing and our understanding of why I am doing it.

There is a Zen story that goes something like this: A university professor went to visit a famous Zen master. While the master quietly served tea, the professor talked about Zen. The master poured the visitor's cup to the brim, and then kept pouring. The professor watched the overflowing cup until he could no longer restrain himself. "It's overfull! No more will go in!" the professor blurted. "You are like this cup," the master replied, "How can I show you Zen unless you first empty your cup?"

My friend Danny Dreyer, creator of ChiRunning and ChiWalking, uses a similar metaphor when he observes that our minds can either be like a pancake or a bagel. Syrup soaks into the former and runs off the latter, the way information, ideas, and insights can enter our minds or not, depending on how receptive or closed they are.

Awareness is a process of opening and deepening; we open to ourselves, to each other, to larger social groups, and to the greater, interdependent whole. In this chapter we will focus

FIGURE 3

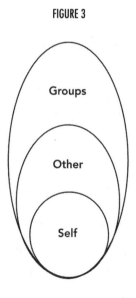

on awareness at three distinct, albeit related, levels or spheres: awareness of self, awareness of self in relationship to others, and awareness of self in relationship to groups.

Awareness of self is essential because, to the extent that we are distinct, individual selves, all awareness begins with self-awareness. "To thine own self be true," wrote Shakespeare, "and it must follow, as the night the day, Thou canst not then be false to any man." Similarly, Carl Jung wrote: "Your vision will become clear only when you can look into your own heart. Who looks outside, dreams; who looks inside, awakens." To be true to ourselves and to awaken, we must first know who we are, how we are oriented, how we respond to events—both internal and external, and how we perceive and embody the relationship between the self and the larger, interdependent whole of which we are a reflection.

Finding our "genius" is among the greatest opportunities and challenges we face. While natural talent certainly helps, cultivating that talent and applying it with focus and energy are essential. Cultivating conscious awareness catalyzes connection with our calling and activates our potential. It begins by tuning in to our interior experience and manifests through the process of carrying conscious awareness into our relationships.

Awareness of self in relationship to others is critical because we do not exist in a vacuum, and to consciously work with others and serve the greater good through our work we must understand the dynamics of our relationships with others: how we perceive, influence, and affect them, and how they perceive, influence, and affect us. We may have our vision of the way things are meant to work, but we cannot manifest our vision alone. Collaborators, customers, vendors, investors, and others may all be required for us to turn our ideas into realities. How we relate to them and they to us will inform our ability to realize our aspirations to be Working for Good.

Awareness of self in relationship to groups is relevant because groups are the fundamental level of social organization. We live in families, work in teams, belong to social organizations, and otherwise coexist with others in groups. In the context of conscious business, we identify and co-create with the interdependent stakeholder groups mentioned earlier, which can include customers, team members, investors, vendors, local community members, and others. Integrating multiple perspectives and interests of diverse groups and facilitating collaboration are essential to building a successful business or effecting change in any context.

To become a conscious entrepreneur or change agent through our work and to successfully navigate the unfolding process of creating an enterprise in an ever-evolving context, we need to be able to change the very fabric of our thought— in our relationships to ourselves, others, and the world.

AWARENESS: WHAT IT IS AND HOW IT WORKS

When you look into a pool of water, if the water is still, you can see the moon reflected.

If the water is agitated, the moon is fragmented and scattered. It's harder to see the true moon.

Our minds are like that. When our minds are agitated, we cannot see the true world.

— TRADITIONAL ZEN SAYING

Let's use an image of a high mountain lake as a metaphor for the mind. Its surface is sometimes clear and calm, other times opaque and rough. Sometimes warm, other times cold, even frozen. Similarly, under the surface it may be clear and calm or murky and turbulent. It is always made of the same essential element, water, but displays vastly different appearances and character. It reflects sun, clouds, birds, stars, and moon, even our own image as we look into it, but it remains essentially unchanged.

Our minds are similar, in that sensations, feelings, thoughts, and intuitions pass through and may stir up our minds for a while the way water is stirred by wind, rain, and other phenomena, only to settle again. These elements transform the lake—by adding new water, or by changing its temperature or particulate constituents. Water remains water, but *how* it is water varies. It may be safe to drink, or not. It may be eighty or fifty degrees. It may be crystal clear or filled with floating microorganisms.

In the same way, our mind is a mind—with the capacity to do what minds do and be what minds are—but what it carries, how it appears, and even how it functions are affected by what we experience and how we integrate these experiences.

Awareness involves observing and recognizing what we are sensing, feeling, thinking, and intuiting—watching our mind as it relates to our experiences. And by watching with detachment and compassion, making time and space to settle any agitation, we can integrate our experiences and reorganize ourselves in a meaningful way. A settled mind sees more clearly and responds more creatively to circumstances than a turbulent one.

Let's take a moment to experience what I mean by observing and recognizing what is going on inside. Take a deep breath. And another. And a third. How did your awareness of your breathing change after you read these words and—if you did—after you took these three breaths? What, if anything, did you feel in your body? How was your experience of your body different in those moments from when you read the preceding paragraph? I trust you get the idea: when you observe your experience and your response to it, you have a different experience.

Given the incredible magnitude of sensory input and emotional and mental activity we usually process, much of our awareness is unconscious. That is, we don't recognize what we are sensing, feeling, thinking, or intuiting, or how it affects us. The awareness I am referring to in this book, and in discussing Working for Good, is conscious awareness—awareness we explicitly recognize and purposefully act upon. It builds in stages and can increase over time as we practice and learn from it. This is not to presume that all that is conscious is correct or good by any absolute, or even relative, standard. But what is conscious is something we can reflect on, share with others, and actively interact with in order to change or manifest. Awareness, like writing a book, creating a product, or building a business, is iterative. Awareness builds awareness. And our decisions and actions based on our awareness change us and change the world.

Our focus here is on practices that give us the freedom to consciously choose how we respond to our experiences and circumstances. The exercises in this chapter are designed to help you observe how you respond to your experiences, other people, and groups, and to cultivate your ability to turn on the switch of awareness—on demand, on the spot, and in the heat of your daily affairs—so you can see challenges and dramas (including disappointments over people missing deadlines, the stresses of unexpected changes in the economy, conflicts between coworkers, and new demands from clients) for what they are: passing phenomena, much like passing clouds reflecting on the surface of a lake, and not an eternal state or essential condition of who you are. With practice, you can begin to see that you are not your sensations, feelings, thoughts, or intuitions, and you can increasingly influence the ground of your being, the quality of your relationships, and the world you manifest with everyone else.

This opens you to a broad range of options and opportunities, fostering creativity, innovation, and receptivity to others. It also reduces stress and improves your overall health and well-being.

Exercise: Opening to Awareness

Among the most basic and effective practices for building conscious awareness is mindfulness meditation, also called insight meditation or Vipassana. Mindfulness practice builds conscious awareness of what is happening, how we perceive it, and how we respond to it in the moment.

Let's do an exercise in what I mean by awareness and mindfulness; then we can reflect on it. You can do this in a few ways. You can read it, then close your eyes and do it; or you can have someone read it to you. You can also do the exercise with your eyes open as you read.

With your eyes open or closed, observe what your body feels like while you are reading or listening to this. Observe how it feels to hold this book in your hands. Are you holding it loosely or tightly? Is one hand holding it differently from the other hand? Is there anything else you notice?

How does the way you are holding the book affect your arms and shoulders? Are your arms bent comfortably or uncomfortably? Are your shoulders relaxed or hunched, even slightly? If so, let your shoulders drop. Notice whether there is a difference in the way the book feels in your hands now.

How are you breathing? Are you breathing in a deep, relaxed manner or in a shallow, constricted one? Are you breathing into the top of your lungs or all the way down? Is your belly moving as you breathe?

How does the book feel in your hands now? And how do your arms and shoulders feel?

Pay attention to your breathing again. Take a few slow, deep breaths. Feel the sensation of the book in your hands again. Feel your arms and shoulders. Now feel your breathing, the book in your hands, your arms and shoulders, all at the same time.

What are the differences between how you feel now and how you did when you began? What differences are there in how the book feels in your hands? What difference is there in your arms and shoulders? In your breathing? Is there anything else you notice?

Take a deep breath or two. Let your body release. And, if they are closed, open your eyes.

This simple mindfulness practice is a gateway to a whole unfolding world of new insights and experiences, with profound implications for your work and your life. We'll build on mindfulness practice in a moment, and again as we move into the other skills of Working for Good.

If you are like me, you might be feeling a little impatient. "I've got a lot to do. Slowing down, watching the way I am holding a book, and breathing are not going to help me get it all done!" I would have felt the same way at some point (and probably still do sometimes), but increasingly I find that slowing down and observing in this way actually accelerates my productivity, because it gives me useful information, releases tension and blocked energy, and creates space for new insights and creativity. It also lays the groundwork for better listening and communication, which deepens both relationship and collaboration.

In the words of Dr. Seuss, "This may not seem very important, I know. But it *is*. So I'm bothering telling you so." Let's remember that the reason we are cultivating awareness is to support us in being more present and effective in our work so that we can manifest our highest potential and most inspiring aspirations.

A useful step in learning and applying mindfulness practice and cultivating awareness begins with recognizing that we experience and relate to the world through different "channels." We tend to have a primary channel we experience and relate through, while employing the others as well. Awareness of these channels and our relationship to them is essential to cultivating and applying awareness, in general and in the context of work. The four channels we will explore here are senses, emotions, thoughts, and intuitions.

Pioneering psychologist Carl Jung based his system of personality types on these four channels, defining four core personality types: sensate, feeling, thinking, and intuiting. These align closely with the four factors of mindfulness the Buddha articulated, which—given twenty-five hundred years of empirical evidence, including significant contemporary scientific and medical validation—supports using this approach as a basis for mapping and tracking our awareness.

Sensate types relate to sensory stimuli and perceive the world principally through their senses. Feeling types perceive the world from the heart, tend to be emotional, and consider values in assessing their experience. Thinking types relate to the world from their heads, employing rational analysis, and tend to be less emotional and more detached. Intuitive types experience the world through gut feelings, inspiration, and insight. Intuition is the source of innovation, inspiration, and creativity.

We all embody some degree of all of these personality types and tend to exhibit one more than the others, and each of them differently in different contexts.

Tuning In to Sensations

I don't know about you, but when I enter a room, in business or otherwise, the first thing I do is not think or feel but observe and sense. My eyes, ears, sense of balance, sense of relationship to other people and things, and sense of my own body fill me with information, which then informs how I feel, what I think, and what I intuit about what is going on and what might happen next.

Our bodies are incredibly intelligent. While we believe we think with our minds, our bodies are great receptors, interpreters, and projectors of experience. They continually read the terrain for us and inform our awareness. They sense our physical orientation and relationship to other bodies. They sense temperature and sustain our balance, and they can detect when our sense of balance is challenged. They carry memories and experiences, and without our conscious intervention they respond to subtle signals to protect and guide us. We can learn a lot if we pay attention to how our bodies feel and respond to our thoughts and actions, and to external circumstances and other people. And we can apply this intelligence to how we move in our work.

Exercise: Tuning In to Sensations—Body Sweeping

The purpose of this exercise is to build on the first exercise of holding the book and then go more directly and deeply into the body. As with the first exercise and all of the exercises in this book, you can do this with your eyes open or closed.

Begin by standing up. Bend your knees slightly. Take a few deep breaths.

Feel your jaw and your shoulders drop as gravity does its work.

Now imagine there is a string coming out of the top of your head with a helium balloon attached to it. It is gently extending your spine upward. There is no great pulling, just a gentle upward movement. Your jaw and shoulders are dropping, your spine extending.

Now feel another string coming out of your tail-bone, extending downward as though it were a tree root reaching into the earth for moisture and nutrition.

Roots are reaching downward, spine extending upward. Your breathing is steady, calm, and deep.

Now focus on the top of your head, and as you breathe, become aware of how the top of your head feels. Keep breathing as you feel your scalp, your temples, and the back of your head.

Now feel your ears, inside and out. Breathe.

Feel your eyes, nose, and mouth. Breathe. Feel your whole face.

Feel your neck. Breathe.

Feel the base of your neck and your shoulders, front and back.

Feel your upper back and your armpits. Feel your upper chest. Feel your breath.

Feel your heart. Feel your lungs. Breathe. Feel your chest open and expand.

Feel your ribs, sides, belly, and lower back, as though there is a soft ring around your body that is slowly sliding down it. Breathe.

Feel the bottom of your spine, pelvis, hips, and the insides of your legs. Breathe.

Feel your thighs, down to your knees. Feel your calves and shins. Feel your breath moving down your body.

Feel your ankles, the tops of your feet, your toes. Feel the soles of your feet on the ground. Breathe into the soles of your feet.

Now bring your attention to your whole body, breathing steadily and deeply.

What do you notice? Do you feel tension or pressure anywhere? Explore it if you do.

Do you feel sensations of hot or cold anywhere? What happens when you direct your attention there? Does your sense of the temperature change? Does anything else happen with your body?

What sounds do you hear? As you tune in to the sounds, do they have any effect on your body?

Do you detect any odors? How do the smells affect you as you tune in to them?

Return your attention to the top of your head, and slowly scan from top to bottom. Notice any sensations as you do.

Take a couple of deep breaths, and open your eyes.

How did that feel? In what ways do you feel different from how you felt before the exercise?

Imagine a situation in your work in which you can tune in to your sensations like that. Perhaps you are on the phone, feeling stress. You can tune in to your body and feel any tension in your body. Breathe into it, and release the tension.

Imagine you have a short break when you can go outside and go through this whole exercise. Do it!

To illustrate body awareness's relevance to work, let's consider this situation for someone we'll call Jen. Jen has just returned to the workplace after six years of focusing on raising her young child, doing volunteer work, and regularly practicing yoga and meditation. She is thoughtful, bright, and very self-aware, but not very experienced in business—and a little self-conscious about it. She is working in a fast-moving "green" start-up owned by friends.

Jen is in a very intense planning meeting, where ideas and arms and hands are moving fast. Since she is relatively new, many of the ideas are foreign to her and she doesn't have the full context. She knows that this kind of meeting provides a great opportunity to learn a lot about the business and about her colleagues, since it is covering the whole picture, yet she feels herself starting to glaze over, overwhelmed by all the information and energy.

She notices that her chest is tight and her breath shallow, which she knows indicate fear and insecurity. She focuses on the tightness and slowly takes a few deep breaths, right into the tight area. She feels some tightness in her back now that her chest is starting to relax, and she does the same thing there. After a few minutes of this, she notices that everything seems to have slowed down and she can track the flow of ideas, and she starts to get a deeper sense of who these people are she is working with. She even asks a few questions. By the time the meeting is over, she feels like she is part of the team, and feels like others see her that way too.

Maybe you can recall or imagine a situation in your work where you had a similar experience. Imagine you are in a challenging conversation and you can notice what your body is sensing, how it is responding, and how it shifts as you pay attention to the sensations. On a more basic level, how often are you aware that you are thirsty? What do you do? And how often are you aware when you need to stretch or move? When you are tired? When you might be on the verge of getting sick? How do you respond to these sensations? And what is the effect of your response?

Our bodies trigger emotions, which trigger thoughts, which in turn drive our responses and actions. If we can notice our body sensations, observe them, and let them move through us, we can tap into the emotions connected with them and gradually unravel the stories built upon the emotions.

How Do You Feel?

A Zen student came to Bankei and complained: "Master, I have an ungovernable temper. How can I cure it?"

"You have something very strange," replied Bankei. "Let me see what you have."

"Just now I cannot show it to you," replied the other.

"When can you show it to me?" asked Bankei.

"It arises unexpectedly," replied the student.

"Then," concluded Bankei, "it must not be your own true nature. If it were, you could show it to me at any time. When you were born you did not have it, and your parents did not give it to you. Think that over." [1]

For many of us, emotions are difficult to recognize and understand. And when we do feel them, they can be over-whelming and all-encompassing. As this story illustrates, we are not our emotions; they are states that pass through us, even if they completely capture us. Emotions are important barometers of our internal condition and indicators of the effects our circumstances and others have on us. Equally important, our emotions can have profound effects on others and dramatically influence relationships and the way events unfold. When the boss comes to work in a bad mood, visibly angry and agitated, fear, anxiety, and stress often permeate the office. When she comes to work with a positive, friendly attitude, inquiring about people's weekend or well-being, a different atmosphere pervades the space.

One of the reasons we cultivate conscious awareness is to maintain perspective in relation to our emotions, so that they do not overwhelm us and drive reactive, unconscious behaviors, such as passive-aggressive expressions of unex-pressed feelings, subtle racist or sexist put-downs, shaming, blaming, or other belittling behaviors. Another reason is so that we can understand the messages our feelings are trying to communicate to us, in order to draw on their insight and wisdom. Tuning into and consciously relating to our emotions can profoundly influence our actions and their consequences, such as owning and expressing our fears and concerns, acknowledging a decision to exercise our authority, and exploring our unconscious prejudices. Emotional intelligence—the ability to skillfully relate to our emotions—has become widely recognized as one of the most significant attributes of an effective leader.

Exercise: How Do You Feel?

Since facing emotions directly is difficult for many of us, one way to tap into them is through an indirect approach, by starting in a different "channel," such as body sensations, breathing, or visualization. In this exercise, you'll read scenarios that evoke emotions, observe what you feel, and name those feelings. To make it easier to access them, we'll give you the option to first observe body sensations and move into feelings from there.

Sit or stand comfortably. If you are standing, bend your knees slightly. Take a few deep breaths. Feel your jaw and your shoulders drop as gravity does its work. With each inhale, feel your spine lengthen. With each exhale, feel your shoulders and jaw drop. Quickly scan your body to sense whether there is any tension. If you find some, breathe into it and observe it. Then move on.

Imagine a butterfly breaking out of the chrysalis, struggling to get its wings free. Pushing with its feet, pulling its body forward, lifting its wet wings upward, still stuck. Struggling, moving. All of a sudden, release! Wings free, then open, slowly flapping and drying in the air. Followed by takeoff!

What do you feel when you read that? Perhaps you might call it suspense, followed by elation. Are there other words you would use?

Where in your body, if anywhere, do you observe sensations? What are they like? Do you notice changes in them as you read through the story? Read it again, and notice any body sensations. When you identify one, ask yourself what emotion it connects to. Feel that emotion. Breathe with it.

As you read the following story, see if you can observe your breath and any body sensations that might arise:

You are at your desk, focusing on a challenging project you have been working on for weeks, and you need to finish it by the end of the day. You are finally in the groove and know that you will make the deadline. You hear a knock on the door and say, "Come in." A colleague or coworker enters, looking harried and hurried. "Help!" he says. "We've got a problem and we need you right away." "But—" you think or say. "Let's go. Now!" he says.

What do you feel after reading?

Reflecting on the story, did you see it in an image? Did you tighten up anywhere in your body? What other sensations did you experience? Read it again and notice any body sensations. When you identify one, ask yourself what emotion it connects to. Feel that emotion. Breathe with it.

Take a few deep breaths and observe what feelings and sensations move through you.

Images, scenes, stories, memories, concerns, and the people and activity around us stir up emotions. And we carry these emotions with us into our work and interactions.

To further illustrate this point, here's a story based on a recent exchange I had with a colleague. Let's call her Beth. Beth is a highly dedicated and productive person, committed to doing good in the world through her work in ways that create win-win opportunities for everyone involved. She is very good at taking strong positions and relentlessly defending them; she expects consistency and excellence from everyone around her; and she supports them in every way she can think of.

In this particular situation, facing an upcoming deadline, Beth was feeling disappointed with and critical of a coworker, who seemed to be falling short of the mark, not responding quickly enough to requests for action, and focusing on projects and tasks other than the one with the looming deadline. When I heard this, I asked Beth if she would take a minute to look at her concerns with the coworker.

After she agreed, I asked her to take a couple of breaths, which she did. Then I acknowledged that she was under tremendous stress; her assistant was in the hospital and, in addition to the deadline in question she had several others of similar significance. Also, a very dear friend had recently died, and work was being done on her house, creating disruption.

I asked her to check in with her body and to see what was going on. She noticed tension in various places. I encouraged her to breathe and feel the tension. As she did, I invited her to sense the stress she was feeling and how it was building into anxiety. And to keep breathing. Little by little, Beth slowed down and was able to identify her fear and anxiety about not getting everything done in time.

As she released the tension, she talked about the situation with our coworker and told a different story about it: how the coworker was probably right on track. The things she had not responded to could probably wait a couple of days, and given that she was going to be "full on, twenty-four seven" for four days the coming week, it was probably good that she was shifting her focus somewhat. Beth felt relieved and we moved on to other topics.

The point of this story is that when she began with awareness of what was going on inside herself, Beth could relax, see things differently, and realize that the issue was not with her coworker, but within herself.

Imagine a similar situation for yourself: one in which you are getting worked up about something, anxious, tense, and critical of someone you are working with. Now tune in to your body and your breath. Take a few deep breaths. Identify places in your body where you are feeling tense. Breathe into them. Let them release. Now go back to the situation in your mind. In what ways does it look or feel different?

Our emotions can be useful monitors of external conditions and barometers for our internal condition, but they do not have to define or control us. By paying attention to them, we can both hear and express the useful messages they convey, and avoid being carried away by them. When we are not aware of what is going on inside ourselves, we are often not aware of how we respond to our circumstances or the effects of our actions on others.

Thinking About Our Thinking

Two monks strolling along a river on their way home to their monastery came across a young woman crying by the bank of the river, where the bridge had given in. Distraught that she could not cross to meet her family for an important event, she asked the monks if they could help her across. Thinking of the vows he had made not to touch women, the younger of the monks declared, "You must know that we are prohibited from doing so."

The other, elder monk, feeling compassion for the woman, invited her to climb onto his back and carried her across the river. After leaving the grateful woman on the other shore, he returned to his companion and they continued on their way back to the monastery.

Clearly agitated, the other monk proclaimed with great disdain, about an hour later, "How could you break the rules of our order and carry that woman?"

The other responded, "She was in great need and that was an act of compassion. I carried her across and left her on the other shore. It seems as though you are still carrying her."[2]

Our minds are amazing things. They can conjure up visions and create whole worlds, which we manifest into reality. Mind plays an essential role for entrepreneurs and change agents, as visioning and then pursuing a vision to its fruition is one of their core attributes. Mind is the activator. It is also a great trickster, making us believe that everything it conjures up is true, and it will tell us stories that can lead us into difficult terrain, down dead-end paths, and into confrontations with others and their stories.

The essence of being conscious is our ability to observe our minds and free ourselves from mental conditioning, prejudices, and limiting thought patterns and to respond openly, authentically, and creatively to the present moment. Given the complexities and endless challenges we face in our work, it is an excellent platform for cultivating conscious awareness of our thinking. Designing and developing new products, organizing our working teams, managing funding and finances, and countless other functions in business require high-level, focused thinking and thoughtful decisions.

To make conscious decisions, it is essential to develop the ability to observe and openly reflect on our thoughts with detachment and discernment. Like observing sensations and emotions, observing our thoughts helps us slow down and recognize that our thoughts are like moving clouds reflected on the clear lake—passing phenomena rather than fixed and definite objects. We can be carried away by them or we can watch them and choose to go for the ride, or not. Perhaps your phone has stopped ringing, and email volume has slowed down. You've just received last month's data and sales are flat. What's wrong? In a situation like this, we can quickly weave a story. We might start telling ourselves that we have a major problem with dire consequences, and we need to act fast—perhaps to cut costs or push our customers for more business, especially if the overall economic climate is difficult. Taking action may seem like the only thing to do.

But what if we were to observe the process more deeply, collecting and assessing information, asking questions, exploring possible causes? Perhaps we would see a different picture. We could take more thoughtful action, while continuing to observe.

The second approach does not have to be slower than the first, but there is a dramatic difference in how it feels— both to us and to others who are affected. Observing our thoughts and questioning our thinking may not be our first instinct, but it can be profoundly useful, even liberating.

Dallas-based integral business consultant Rand Stagen uses the metaphor of the football coach on the field and the coach in the press box who calls in his perspective from above. These two perspectives are profoundly different and illustrate the value of different perspectives to gaining a full view of the game. Michael Gelb, business consultant and author of *How to Think Like Leonardo da Vinci*, reflects on Leonardo's practice of looking at things from multiple perspectives. When Leonardo prepared to render something in a painting, he would sketch it from at least three different perspectives; then he would hold each sketch in front of a mirror to see even more perspectives, and then he would ask someone else to critique his sketches for still another perspective. One of the greatest geniuses of all time deeply understood the value of expanding one's field of view. In doing so he created some of the most powerful art and most creative inventions of all time.

Exercise: Observing Our Thoughts

Regardless of our personality type or intelligence profile, we all think. And thoughts typically stream through our minds almost incessantly. Since we are not usually aware of most of the thoughts that pass by, we often get caught or carried away by them. This exercise is designed to shine a light on your thoughts so you can see how they run rampant through your mind and mitigate their influence—by learning how to observe them and let them pass without being pulled in one direction or another.

Sit or stand comfortably. If you are standing, bend your knees slightly. Take a few deep breaths. Feel your jaw and your shoulders drop as gravity does its work. With each inhale, feel your spine lengthen. With each exhale,

WORKING FOR GOOD

feel your shoulders and jaw drop. Quickly scan your body to sense whether there is any tension. If you find some, breathe into it and observe it. Then move on.

Notice any thought that presents itself. Breathe. Relax. And watch the thought. Don't try to hold it, don't try to push it away; just watch it. And continue to watch it until it passes away and another thought takes its place. Do this for a while, until you are ready to stop.

What did you notice? Did you make the thoughts happen, or did they appear by themselves? Did you find yourself getting caught up in any of the thoughts? Did they start you on a journey of creating a story?

Thoughts are mischievous and truly out of control. They come when they want to, and they go where they want to, often taking us along for the ride— triggering emotions and building thoughts upon thoughts that create stories about ourselves, others, and the world. While these stories are sometimes useful and even accurate, they are often misleading and unproductive.

By practicing mindful observation of our thoughts— in meditation and in our daily lives—we can slow down the torrent of thoughts and stories and learn to observe them with some detachment, not taking them so seriously or believing everything they want us to believe. Then we can assess them critically, consider other information and perspectives, and form opinions and make decisions more purposefully.

Three monks decided to practice meditation together. They sat by the side of a lake and closed their eyes in concentration. Then suddenly, the first one stood up and said, "I forgot my mat." He stepped miraculously onto the water in front of him and walked across the lake to their hut on the other side.

When he returned, the second monk stood up and said, "I forgot to put my other underwear out to dry." He, too, walked calmly across the water and returned the same way. The third monk watched the first two carefully in what he decided must be the test of his own abilities. "Is your learning so superior to mine? I, too, can match any feat you two can perform," he declared loudly and rushed to the water's edge to walk across it. He promptly fell into the deep water.

Undeterred, he climbed out of the water and tried again, only to sink into the water. Yet again he climbed out and yet again he tried, each time sinking. This went on for some time as the other two monks watched.

After a while, the second monk turned to the first and said, "Do you think we should tell him where the stones are?"[2]

So often what we think is not aligned with, or has a limited view of, what is actually going on. We tend to think in the ways we are taught to think, and our thinking is colored by the belief systems we are born into and the ones we cultivate for ourselves. More than individual thoughts, these are complex stories that shape our entire view of and orientation to the world.

For example, we might have grown up in an environment where we did not feel safe. We were taught by that circumstance to approach the world from a place of fear and self-protection, and as such we developed a strong flight-or-fight response. Such a response may have served us at the time, but what if that response continues to get

WORKING FOR GOOD

triggered—in less than truly dangerous situations? In that case, we may take the slightest indication of instability or challenging circumstances as a warning of imminent doom. The story we are telling ourselves, which is rooted in childhood, may cause us to act in a manner that is out of proportion to the current situation. With more detached observation, combined with direct inquiry and investigation, we may discover a completely different dynamic unfolding than the one we envisioned.

Before we go running into the lake, it is a good idea to check our view of the water and actually look into it to see what is going on!

Just Knowing: Intuition and Inspiration

My friend and colleague Michael Strong tells a story about a hike he took on a high plateau in Alaska. When he got to the edge of the plateau, he watched with awe as clouds popped into existence out of thin air. Knowing can be like this. Ideas, understandings, whole-being awareness can pop into existence without a direct relationship to a sensation, feeling, or thought.

Intuition is elusive, intangible, and not something we are typically supported to cultivate. Our culture and institutions emphasize cognitive thinking and value logical and verbal intelligence. And while they value our ability to think in pictures, patterns, and structures to some extent, they do not give great credence to knowing without knowing *why*. Validating our knowing with logical explanations, substantive material justifications, and even emotional rationale goes much further than "I just know it." But "just knowing it" can be as real, valid, and valuable as any other way of knowing. In fact, for some of us, and at some times for all of us, it is the primary and most valid way of knowing. In his bestselling book *Blink: The Power of Thinking Without Thinking*, Malcolm Gladwell celebrates the power of instant judgments and makes a compelling case for training our senses and minds to focus on the most relevant information to facilitate ever more skillful intuitive and instant decision-making.

Listening to intuition—the inner sense of just knowing—can be profoundly important. While it did not happen in the context of business, I remember this instance where my intuitive sense saved my life.

During the summer before my senior year in college, I took a cross-country motorcycle trip. A few hours into the first day of the trip, I was riding through Harrisburg, Pennsylvania, during rush hour on an interstate highway. One of the two lanes heading west was closed and traffic was bumper-to-bumper, moving at around 40 miles an hour. Right behind me was a large semi. All of a sudden, with no external signals to indicate it, I sensed that I was in danger, and without thinking, I pulled around the pylons into the closed right lane. As I was doing so, the semi behind me surged forward into the space I had occupied and shook as though it was in an earthquake. It settled back down and slowed down enough to make space for me again, and I returned to the space in front of it, unconcerned now and "knowing" that I was not at risk. I don't know if the driver fell asleep or was otherwise unconscious for a moment, or what happened. All I knew at the time was that I had to move or I would be killed. And I also knew that after that moment of danger, I was not at further risk. How did I know this? I sure don't know. But it illustrates how we can just know something and effectively respond to this knowing in ways that are essential to our well-being and success.

Recall a situation in which you had a similar "felt sense" of something you needed to do to avoid danger or, conversely, grasp an opportunity. Imagine it now in your mind and reflect on it for a moment. Notice whether there are any sensations or emotions that come up for you as you reflect on this experience.

Many of the biggest career decisions I have made in my life were based on an experience of just knowing, in the moment, without analyzing information, sensations, or feelings. I simply recognized that this was something I needed to pursue or choose to do.

Entrepreneurs, artists, and change agents often rely on intuition as inspiration. Symphonies, paintings, new technologies, and other works of creative expression often appear to their creators in a flash, fully realized in their minds, even if it takes years for them to materialize what they saw, working until they make intuitive "just knowing" a physical reality.

AWARENESS OF SELF

The greatest discovery of my age is that men can change their circumstances by changing the attitude of their mind.

—WILLIAM JAMES

To continue our exploration and cultivation of awareness, let's tune in to a few elements of self-awareness and different ways of looking at self.

First, let's recall that we each relate to ourselves, others, and the world in different ways. We take things in differently from the way others do, and we learn, process information, and express ourselves differently as well. Howard Gardner defines these different ways of relating to the world as *multiple intelligences* and has identified nine primary ones. Some are analytic, using our cognition; others are introspective, fostering self-knowledge; and still others are interactive, facilitating connection to others. I introduce the nine intelligences here to open and expand our sense of who we are.

- *Verbal/linguistic intelligence* is based on our facility for learning and expressing ourselves through the spoken and written word.
- *Logical/mathematical intelligence* is based on our ability to learn and express ourselves through reasoning and problem-solving.
- *Visual/spatial intelligence* reflects our ability to learn and express ourselves visually and to organize ideas spatially. With visual/spatial intelligence, we see things in our minds and express our visions.
- *Musical/rhythmic intelligence* is based on our ability to learn and express through patterns, rhythms, and music. This includes the ability to recognize patterns through all of our senses.
- *Bodily/kinesthetic intelligence* means learning and expressing ourselves through interaction with our environment, including contact with other people. It reflects understanding through concrete experience, movement, and physical orientation.
- *Intrapersonal intelligence* means the ability to learn and express ourselves through feelings, values, and attitudes. This is also an aspect of emotional intelligence.
- *Interpersonal intelligence* reflects our ability to learn and express ourselves through interaction with others.

- *Naturalist intelligence* involves learning and expressing ourselves through classification, categories, and hierarchies—not limited to the study of nature, but applied to any phenomenon.
- *Existential intelligence* is our ability to learn and express ourselves through seeing the "big picture" and considering the relationship between ourselves and the greater whole. This intelligence applies the theoretical to practical applications.

Clearly, we all embody each of these intelligences in varying degrees and in different combinations. Social intelligence, our ability to effectively interact with others, for instance, requires a combination of intelligences, including verbal, intrapersonal, and interpersonal. And depending upon whom we are engaging with, the combination of intelligences will vary in order to connect with others' orientation and style.

Exercise: Reflection on Intelligence

Let's take a moment to reflect on these nine intelligences, each in turn. After you read the brief description below for each one, close your eyes for a moment and see if anything comes up for you: a sensation, a feeling, a thought, a knowing—whatever comes up. Reflect for a moment on the questions: "What do you think about your strength with this intelligence? What have others said about your talent with this intelligence?" Then rate your intelligence on the scale below: not very developed, fairly well developed, or highly developed. There are no right or wrong assessments and, clearly, this is not an objective or scientific exercise. It is meant simply to tune you in even more to your orientation and self-perception, and perhaps to spark a curiosity that will lead you to explore this question more deeply and cultivate your multiple intelligences.

First, take a few deep breaths. With each inhale, feel your spine lengthen. With each exhale, feel your shoulders and jaw drop. Check to see that you are comfortable with how you are seated, and proceed.

Verbal/linguistic intelligence: Word smart

❑ Not very developed
❑ Fairly well developed
❑ Highly developed

Logical/mathematical intelligence: Logic smart

❑ Not very developed
❑ Fairly well developed
❑ Highly developed

Visual/spatial intelligence: Picture smart

❑ Not very developed
❑ Fairly well developed
❑ Highly developed

Musical/rhythmic intelligence: Pattern smart

❑ Not very developed
❑ Fairly well developed
❑ Highly developed

Bodily/kinesthetic intelligence: Body smart

❑ Not very developed
❑ Fairly well developed
❑ Highly developed

Intrapersonal intelligence: Self smart
❑ Not very developed
❑ Fairly well developed
❑ Highly developed

Interpersonal intelligence: People smart
❑ Not very developed
❑ Fairly well developed
❑ Highly developed

Naturalist intelligence: Order smart
❑ Not very developed
❑ Fairly well developed
❑ Highly developed

Existential intelligence: Deep question smart
❑ Not very developed
❑ Fairly well developed
❑ Highly developed

Excellent. Take a few breaths and reflect on this exercise. What, if anything, came up for you? Any overall sensations? Emotions? Thoughts? Insights?

If you are interested in exploring the idea of multiple intelligences and assessing your own more deeply, you can find many assessment tools online, and you can read *Frames of Mind: The Theory of Multiple Intelligences* by Howard Gardener.

Let's consider a situation where different intelligences come into play. The context is a conflict between different teams working together to launch an important new product. The launch date is quickly approaching, and things are not quite on track. One team is focused on the design and promotion of the product, the other on production and administration. Ann is a lead player on the production/administration team. She is highly logical and sharp as a tack—she has the facts down solidly. Bob is a leader on the design/promotion team. He is creative, emotional, and passionate. The interaction between the two represents the conflict between the teams and the challenge for the collaborative effort.

Ann holds up the numbers and claims that the creative team is over budget and jeopardizing the product's opportunity to succeed. Bob bemoans the "handcuffs" Ann and her team put on him and his team as responsible for compromising their ability to make important design modifications, and thus putting the ultimate success of the product at risk. One focuses on the numbers, the other on design function and aesthetics. Both Ann and Bob have a significant part to play in the success of the product launch, but they relate to the world and to each other in different ways.

Imagine how this situation could shift if Ann, Bob, or both of them employed a high level of intrapersonal intelligence, exercising empathy and considerate listening, and if they employed verbal intelligence, carefully choosing their words to reflect their perspective while considering the impact on the other person. And what if they could come from the vantage point of existential intelligence and really see the big picture, opening up new possibilities for resolving the current bottleneck and related conflict?

Recall a challenge—or think of one you are facing now—that you approached with one particular "lens," applying only one of your intelligences. Can you see how other intelligences could have generated or can generate more options for you?

Our intelligence profile informs how we view and relate to ourselves, others, and the world. They influence what we identify with and respond to. We are all intelligent, and we have different levels of each type of intelligence. Throughout the remainder of this book I will refer to these intelligences and use them as a point of reference for cultivating awareness and the other skills of Working for Good: embodiment, connection, collaboration, and integration.

Mindfulness practice is the principal tool we use for cultivating awareness. And the principal framework we use for working with self-awareness is the four temperaments as defined by David Keirsey, whose pioneering work in the 1950s built upon Jung's four types. Keirsey's personality assessment tools are the most widely used in the world.

Temperaments represent an aggregation of attitudes, aptitudes, values, roles, and needs. The foundation of the temperaments is patterns of communication and action: "what we say and what we do." Keirsey defines two principal patterns of communication, concrete versus abstract, and two principal patterns of action, utilitarian versus cooperative. The combinations of these four patterns form the foundation of the four temperaments: Rationals, Artisans, Idealists, and Guardians.

As the name reflects, Rationals are the thinking types. They tend to be logical, pragmatic, and strategic. They love abstract concepts and work to create practical applications of them. They process facts well, seek knowledge, and yearn for achievement. They value efficiency and thrive on solving problems. Albert Einstein, Bill Gates, and Thomas Jefferson are examples Keirsey gives of Rationals.

Artisans relate through the senses. What is tangible is real to the Artisan. They tend to be spirited—independent, fun-loving, playful, spontaneous, impulsive, and adventurous. They are often open, charming, and generous. John F. Kennedy, Bruce Lee, Amelia Earhart, and Madonna are examples of Artisans.

Idealists are the intuitive types. They are enthusiastic, idealistic seekers, looking for meaning, personal growth, spiritual development, and deep relationships. Unlike Artisans, they focus more on what can be rather than on what is. Examples of Idealists include Mohandas Gandhi, Oprah Winfrey, and Mikhail Gorbachev.

Guardians are the indispensable pillars of society. They tend to be dependable, hard-working, organized, trustworthy, and loyal. They know and respect rules and follow them comfortably. Examples of Guardians include George Washington, Queen Elizabeth, and Harry Truman.

Here are four character profiles to further illustrate the temperaments. We'll meet these four people again later on.

- *Rational:* Jack is a serial tech entrepreneur, with a new start-up focused on new tools for social networking. He is highly competitive, loves to read, and runs marathons. He leads a strong management team, in which teamwork and competition coexist. While seemingly aloof, he is a strong and thoughtful leader.

- *Artisan:* Jocelyn is a singer-songwriter and performance artist, building her career through online communities and playing live at festivals, yoga studios, and other cultural gathering places. She incorporates media, installations, and theater in her performances. Her music focuses on social issues and she supports many causes through her art.

- *Idealist:* Sue is a social entrepreneur who is catalyzing a new program designed to deliver empowerment education to inner-city youth. She believes that business is a path for spiritual growth and service, and that business can serve the higher aspirations of humanity. She is organizing her innovative social program as a for-profit business, as she believes that idealism is sustainable.
- *Guardian:* Evan is project manager at a green tech company. Trained as a computer science engineer, he manages the development of energy management systems for homes, offices, and factories. He keeps a team of systems engineers, interface designers, and salesmen on the same page, on track, and within budget. He thrives on seeing things work well and according to plan.

Take a moment to reflect on these four characters. How do you relate to them? Is there one you identify with more than the others? Can you see aspects of yourself in all of them?

"Musicians must make music, artists must paint, poets must write if they are to be ultimately at peace with themselves. What human beings can be, they must be. They must be true to their own nature," wrote Abraham Maslow. Our temperament reflects our inclinations: how we are most likely to think, communicate, and act. Fish swim, birds fly, inventors invent, leaders lead. Understanding our intelligence profile and our temperament—finding what we excel at, cultivating our skill, and employing it in our work—is a key to success, happiness, and well-being, and is critical to making a difference while flourishing in business.

To promote happiness and well-being, Martin Seligman advises us to know our signature strengths and use them as much as possible. According to Anne Marie Burgoyne, program director at the Draper Richards Foundation, the most successful social entrepreneurs are self-reflective and self-aware. Anne Marie, who funds and supports leading social entrepreneurs, says they know their strengths and passionately apply them in building their enterprises. They also know their weaknesses and surround themselves with people who compensate for them.

Strengths, including intelligence, can take many forms, and every form has its place in Working for Good. We may learn and lead through cognitive intellect, social/emotional intelligence, intuition, or the ability to make things happen. It may be artistic, visionary, logical, graceful, or some wonderful combination of various attributes that creates a unique character and capacity. Our temperament may be that of the Rational, Artisan, Idealist, or Guardian.

Applying our awareness in order to uncover and cultivate an understanding of our orientation and inclinations is an essential step in moving awareness into action.

Understanding ourselves provides a bridge to understanding others. We can walk around blindfolded, with our hands tied behind our backs (figuratively speaking, of course), or with eyes wide open and arms outstretched. We can know our perspective and how we interpret what we touch—based on our tendencies and by observing what is going on for us in the moment—through mindfulness practice. The tendencies of our intelligence and temperament indicate our likely responses to experiences and situations. Mindfulness practice affords us the opportunity to observe how we process and respond to experiences in the moment, and to choose how we respond—even if it means overriding our tendencies.

AWARENESS OF SELF IN RELATION TO OTHERS

Word spread across the countryside about the wise holy man who lived in a small house atop the mountain. A man from the village decided to make the long and difficult journey to visit him. When he arrived at the house, an old servant inside greeted him at the door. "I would like to see the wise holy man," he said to the servant. The servant smiled and led him inside. As they walked through the house, the man from the village looked eagerly around the house, anticipating his encounter with the holy man. Before he knew it, he had been led to the back door and escorted outside. He stopped and turned to the servant, "But I want to see the holy man!" "You already have," said the old man. "Everyone you may meet in life, even if they appear plain and insignificant . . . see each of them as a wise holy man. If you do this, then whatever problem you brought here today will be solved."[4]

Self-awareness is essential, but it is not enough. In business and in life, relationships are everything. One of the key reasons we cultivate self-awareness is to bring it into relationship with others. To be effective as entrepreneurs and change agents we must engage others to join us in our adventure. And bringing out the best in people and inspiring them to passionately commit themselves requires deep awareness of how we are in relationship to others.

This begins with self-awareness and observing how we think about, feel about, and respond to others, and continues by observing how we affect them and how they respond to us. As we'll explore in more depth in Chapters Four and Five, we build on this awareness to create deeper connection and then collaboration, but it all begins with awareness.

Many of our interactions and relationships with others are colored by the ways we relate to experiences—a reflection of our temperament and intelligences—and by the unconscious baggage we carry in our minds that colors our perceptions of others and influences our behaviors with them. We may be attracted or repulsed by certain people. They may remind us of someone else we love or despise. They may remind us of ourselves or embody some aspects of ourselves we do not care to acknowledge. Or they may simply speak a different language—literally or figuratively—or come from a culture we do not understand or relate to. While these may all be somewhat obvious factors, we often don't consciously consider them when we are engaged in the daily exigencies of doing business and facing people all around us—inside and outside of our organizations—who have a stake in, or an influence on, our success.

Like the practice of being aware of sensations, feelings, thoughts, and intuitions in general, awareness of our relationship to others also begins with slowing down. When we slow down, we can identify the myriad inputs we receive, track our interior landscape, and discern the ways in which our responses to others are unconscious, reactive, or automatic, as opposed to conscious and purposeful. And we can see how our conditioned preconceptions are not necessarily true, or, if they are true, not all that important. Then we can choose consciously, instead of reacting unconsciously, in how we relate to others. And conscious choices, while not always right, tend to be more effective than unconscious reactions.

Perceiving Others
Sensing
The moment we walk into a room, our eyes see the people in it. We smell them. We sense them as we pass by them. Our

bodies respond to their body language, the way they move, and the way they respect or encroach upon our personal space. They provide some of the most intense and challenging, as well as exciting, inputs into our minds. Our awareness is flooded by the information we receive from others.

Recall a time you met a colleague or coworker for the first time. What sensations were you aware of? What did you notice about him or her? How did your body feel? How did these sensations influence the way you related to the person?

The way we process the information our senses receive from the presence of others, and how conscious we are of their effects, are essential to our relationships and our effectiveness in communicating and working with them.

Feeling

A Western Buddhist woman was in India, studying with her teacher. She was riding in a rickshaw-like carriage when she was attacked by a man on the street. In the end, the attacker only succeeded in frightening the woman, but she was quite upset by the event and told her teacher so. She asked him what she should have done—what would have been the appropriate, Buddhist response.

The teacher said very simply, "You should have very mindfully and with great compassion whacked the attacker over the head with your umbrella."[5]

It's no secret that other people are great catalysts for our emotions. Emotions are one way in which we respond to the presence, ideas, and actions of others. I remember the metaphor a colleague once shared with me: Imagine a door in the middle of your chest, with a door knob in it. Other people may knock on the door, even bang on it, but you control the doorknob from the inside. The point is, our emotions are generated from inside ourselves, not from the outside. Many times a day we let our doors fly open with anger, joy, love, disgust, and a myriad other emotions, triggered by our interactions with others as they push our buttons, reflect things we don't want to look at, delight us, or disappoint us. The way we respond to the effect they have on us is a powerful reflection of our awareness practice in action.

Recall a time that you went on a job interview or made a sales presentation to a potential client or financial backer. The moment you met, what feelings came up for you? As you spent more time together, how did your feelings change? How did your feelings inform your presentation and the outcome of the meeting?

In addition to observing the effect others have on us, we can sense how we affect them. In *Primal Leadership*, emotional intelligence champion Daniel Goleman highlights the importance of empathy—the ability to sense others' emotions, understand their perspectives, and act in ways that reflect genuine regard for their interests and concerns—for effective leadership. To lead others, we have to feel them and respond to their feelings: not become therapists for them or get caught up in their feelings, but sense, discern, and consider them in the ways we facilitate movement.

Thinking

Our thoughts love to work their mischievous tricks in our relationships with others. Our minds are certain they are watching out for our best interests, but because they act out of impulse—based on cultural conditioning and often driven by grasping, fear, and uninformed delusion—they can easily misguide us and diminish the possibilities for deeper connection and co-creation.

The stories we tell about people in general, and specific people such as our colleagues and collaborators, deeply influence our relationships with them and the possibilities of what we can create together. Our stories about others also influence their stories about us, as they respond to the way we present ourselves and relate to them. Last summer I was locked in an ongoing struggle with a group of collaborators on a project. We all felt like we were in an unending wrestling match, and we were certain that the "other side" was responsible for initiating and sustaining the conflict. Finally one day, I broke through with the observation that we were coming from vastly different points of view and that it could be helpful if we told one another the story we were carrying about our situation. When the stories were told, we all had a clear understanding of the origin of the conflict and, while we didn't resolve it immediately, we did begin a process that ultimately resulted in its resolution. In a series of subsequent meetings, as we continued to tell our respective stories of our experience working with one another and through the struggle, the stories began to dissolve and a real shift in attitude and behavior ensued. We realized that to a significant extent, the stories we told about one another were self-fulfilling, as our stance toward one another elicited behaviors similar to those in our story. When we shifted the story, the behaviors shifted. We went from a vicious cycle to a virtuous cycle.

Recall a time you had a thought about someone you just met, and it turned out to be wrong. How did that thought influence the way you related to the person? How did your behavior change when you realized that your assumption was not true?

Remember a time when you built a story about a colleague or a client—someone who you were working with or doing business with—that influenced the way you related to the person. How did the story affect the way you related to the person? Was the story positive or negative? If it was positive, how did the person act in ways that reinforced or contradicted your story? If it was negative, how did the individual act in ways that made you question your story?

Sometimes our stories can be accurate and helpful. Other times they can be based on false assumptions or prejudices, create unnecessary conflict, and limit possibilities. They can also set up false expectations and disappointment. Projecting a story onto someone that portrays them as more skillful or advanced than they may be sets a standard they may not yet be prepared to meet, and sets them up for failure in our eyes.

Intuiting

Someone mentions a person's name, one you have never heard before, and you just know that you want or need to meet that person. Ever happen to you? It has happened to me many times. And most of the time, the person in question has added something significant to my life. While the experience may be a composite of sensing, feeling, thinking, and other channels of perception, it comes to us as if it were a cloud popping into existence over a plateau. Even more mysterious than the emergence of a thought, feeling, or sensation, this sense of "just knowing" is beyond rational explanation and apparently transcends sensory input and emotions, as it happens in an instant—fully formed, whole and complete.

Perhaps you can recall a time when you were in a business setting and someone mentioned a name—a new hire, a client, an investor, or a prospective partner—and something in you just knew that this was a significant person. Not only were you going to meet this person, but the two of you would have a significant relationship. What actually happened? Did your experience match your sense of what it would be like?

Or perhaps there was a time when someone from your past came to mind unexpectedly—and you called them, only to find that they had been trying to track you down for months. I did that once and ended up with a job offer I wasn't expecting. It doesn't have to be a person; have you ever had the sense that it was time to return to a project you had been working on for years, only to have the project finally come to fruition? That is certainly my experience with this book!

Each of the four characters we met earlier has a different way of viewing and relating to others. Jack the Rational tends to see how people can serve his interests and the interests of his project. Jocelyn the Artisan tends to see others as playful co-creators. Sue the Idealist often sees others as evolving spiritual beings and partners in co-creating a new reality. Evan the Guardian will likely see people based on how they fit into the order of things and play their role in making things work.

By understanding ourselves, we can understand our relationship to others: how experience of others affects us, and how our responses to these effects influence the way we relate to others.

We can apply the skills of mindful observation to understand and transcend our tendencies, fears, and prejudices and open ourselves to new experiences with others.

AWARENESS OF SELF IN RELATIONSHIP TO GROUPS

The average person at a funeral would rather be in the casket than doing the eulogy.

—JERRY SEINFELD (adapted from an old joke)

One of the most common fears is that of speaking in front of an audience. Groups scare us silly. The only thing scarier than walking down a dark alley and seeing a person lurking in the shadows is seeing a group of people lurking in the shadows. It only makes sense. If you were a member of a tribal community millennia ago and you wandered beyond the safety of your tribal zone and encountered a group from a hostile neighboring tribe, you were in for trouble. The same is true on city streets and in rural neighborhoods to this day, even in the United States of America. Groups form the basic unit of social organization, and they identify themselves in large part by their differences from other groups.

Human beings are social animals. While some of us may prefer to be alone much of the time, most of our lives are spent with other people. We find safety, comfort, identity, and meaning in groups—from families to schools to sports teams to social clubs. We convene and co-create with others in groups.

Business is a team sport and a group process. From our internal employee teams to the interconnected stakeholders in our business ecosystems, groups create a network of human relationships that are essential to the functioning and flourishing of business. If we want to influence this network—to make a difference through business—we have to master the art of working with groups. To do so, we begin by mastering ourselves and applying awareness to our relationships with others; then we continue by applying our awareness practice to our relationship to groups.

To serve as an agent of change in business, we must see how we work within, with, and between groups, and we must learn to conduct ourselves and engage with others to create conscious groups and conscious relationships between groups.

Groups are tough. From social clubs to sports teams, they tend to adhere to fixed norms in order to establish order and regulate behavior. As most of us know from experience, if we happen to have ideas that differ from those prevailing in the group we belong to, we may fare no better than we will with a group of strangers.

In addition to the challenges inherent in groups, we bring to our interaction with groups our own baggage, including our personality, perspectives, strengths, and weaknesses, and our conscious and unconscious feelings about groups.

Depending on our level of social intelligence and temperament, we view and respond to groups in very different ways. Focusing our awareness on our tendencies and our responses in the moment can teach us to be skillful in our interactions with groups and ever more effective in engaging with and managing them.

Technology can be a great tool for facilitating group process, but ultimately what matters is how we use it and the awareness and other skills we bring to the process. In Chapter Four, "Connection," and Chapter Five, "Collaboration," we will explore this in more depth. Here, we will focus on our core relationship to groups and how we can maintain mindfulness as we engage with them.

In the pages ahead, we'll apply awareness skills for each channel—sensing, feeling, thinking, intuiting—to our relationship to groups.

Perceiving Groups

Sensing

You are about to make that speech to an unfamiliar audience. What sensations do you observe in your body? Hair standing up on the back of your neck? Tightness in your belly? Throat a little dry? Or how about entering into a challenging negotiation with a team of adversaries on the other side of the table: how does your body respond to that?

On the other hand, how does it feel to start the week with your team? As you enter the office, how does your body feel? Is energy moving through it? Or is there a tightness in your chest, or some other feeling as you anticipate engaging with your community at work?

Our bodies represent millions of years of evolution: sensing our environment and the other beings in it, assessing danger and opportunity, friend and foe. The sensations in our bodies affect our stance in relation to groups, and they trigger emotions and stories that influence how we relate to groups, both in general and with specific groups.

If we can notice how our bodies respond when we encounter or think about a certain group, we can observe the sensations rather than be unconsciously carried away by them. And we can explore them to see if they hold some important message—a warning of danger, maybe, or a sign of opportunity.

Feeling

Groups can be like prisons, inhibiting initiative and innovation, or like launching pads, generating energy and excitement. They can hold us down or lift us up. Our emotional response to a group is as important as the role the group itself plays. We know that our emotions exert a strong force over us. If they are triggered, they can take off like wildfire, igniting stories and overwhelming us with irrational fear substantiated by seemingly rational stories. Like our sensing body, our emotional responses can limit our ability to effectively interact with groups, yet they also hold meaningful information.

You are about to make a presentation to the sales force of a new distributor of your product. It's your opportunity to engage them as ambassadors for your company. What do you feel? How will these feelings affect your presentation?

Thinking

In his book *Prophets, Profits, and Business*, my friend and colleague Timothy Fort, executive director of the Institute for Corporate Responsibility at George Washington University, tells the following story about "the mad Albanian," based on his experience with a young Albanian refugee he welcomed into his home for three months years ago.

> *The young man explained that practicing religion of any kind was punishable by death in Albania from the time he was a year old. Examples he gave and news stories seem to corroborate that statement. One evening, Petrov (not his real name) asked who God was. I figured that we were in for a long night and started to respond, when he immediately interrupted me by saying that he hated Muslims. He was a Catholic. "But Petrov," I said, "you don't even know what a Catholic is!"*
>
> *"I hate Muslims," he responded.*
>
> *"But why do you hate Muslims?"*

> "Because I am a Catholic."
>
> "What does being a Catholic mean?"
>
> "It means I hate Muslims."
>
> We went around in circles on this issue for quite some time before I gave up, realizing that the entirety of the concept of being Catholic to Petrov was simply that Muslims were his enemy. There wasn't a thread of theological dispute in play. Indeed, he had practiced a "not" strategy. He did not dialogue with Muslims about their religious beliefs. In fact, he was prevented from doing so under penalty of death. The "not" strategy prevented him from even knowing who he was, except to know he was not a Muslim.

This story vividly illustrates the power of social and cultural conditioning. While perhaps not to that degree of irrational intensity, most of us frequently make judgments of people based on appearances, cultural differences, and past experiences. They may remind us of someone we like or don't like, or aspects of ourselves we care not to face. We apply this same process of telling stories and passing judgments based on mental models to groups, organizations, and institutions. And these judgments may be rational—that is, we may go through a thinking process to come to our conclusion—or intuitive, coming to us as a whole, spontaneous knowing from an unknown source.

I remember having a conversation about sponsors with the coproducer of a wonderful film festival; one of my clients was a sponsor. When Starbucks came up in the conversation, she went on a rant about how bad they are, moving into communities and taking over, squeezing all of the independent stores out of business. She went on to say she didn't go to Starbucks but continued to give her business to a local, independent coffee shop. I responded with something like, "So, your favorite shop is still in business. That's great. How is their service since Starbucks came into town?" She responded, "Much better than it ever was. And they've added live music and become even more of a community center." "So," I commented, "it sounds like Starbucks gave them a wake-up call and motivated them to do more and be better at what they do." "Yes, that's true," she observed. "So," I asked, "what's so bad about Starbucks coming into town again?"

As our conversation continued, she acknowledged that she was carrying an anticorporate perspective as part of an unquestioned worldview that she was wearing much like a suit of clothes someone had given her, without questioning where it came from or what it was made of. Because "corporations are bad," she had never thought to consider the many ways in which companies like Starbucks contribute to communities and society overall, providing good jobs for inner-city youth, quality products and services, a new kind of urban community center, and competition to stimulate innovation and elevated service from other coffee shops, tea shops, and other local meeting places.

So much of what we think and how we judge things comes from cultural conditioning and unquestioned assumptions that cut us off from opportunities and lead to decisions based on prejudices rather than facts or other considerations.

If we want to influence a business, we need to understand and skillfully work with its stakeholder groups and balance their interests. Understanding our perspective on and relationship to each stakeholder group provides a foundation for effective engagement. We can always bring awareness to any moment and transcend our preconceptions and prejudices; recognizing them can help us see the need to bring conscious awareness to our decisions and interactions.

Depending upon our temperament, experience, and state of mind, we can have very different views of stakeholder groups. If we appreciate the dynamic play between interests, even in the context of interdependence, we can recognize the way customers call out our excellence, team members bring out our leadership skills—including sensitivity, compassion, and inspiration—investors help us to be responsible and accountable, and vendors cultivate our ability to be fair, balanced, and astute.

If we are in a defensive or negative stance, we might see customers as demanding nuisances, employees as ungrateful and exploitative, investors as greedy and narrow-minded, or vendors as whiny and opportunistic. Undoubtedly, we all have our days when we fall into a negative space like this. The keys to not being caught up in it are to regularly assess our perceptions of the stakeholders and to practice awareness in relationship to them. If we do so, we can work through challenges and opportunities without being handicapped by the baggage of our stories, and we will respond with clarity, creativity, and openness.

Intuiting

How do you vibe a whole group? Or, even more challenging, a whole stakeholder group? The same intuitive sense that we can apply in general, we can apply to our relationship to groups.

If you can, recall a time when you were in a business setting and facing an opportunity—looking for a new client, vendor, or investor—or some other situation where you needed to identify and add a new stakeholder to one of your stakeholder groups. You came across the name of a group to fill your need and had a sense of "this is the one!" What was your actual experience with that group? Did it match up to your sense of what it was going to be? Did you land the client? Hire the vendor? Engage the investor? What happened after you did?

Groups play a big role in our lives and in our businesses. In some respects, groups, more than individuals, are the basic unit of business organization. Awareness practice can play a significant role in our relationship to and collaboration with groups, including whole stakeholder groups in our business ecosystem. By observing our tendencies and our inner experience of groups, we can relate to them and make decisions about and with them more consciously.

As we understand our relationship to groups, we can design our situation to optimize it. For example, my friend Brian Johnson, cofounder of Eteamz.com and Zaadz, put everything he had into building his businesses and catalyzing a team and charged-up customers. After a couple of years of deep engagement, he sold the business and took a year or more of monk-like sabbatical. Now, during his retreat, he's building a more solitary business called PhilosophersNotes. com—reflecting his natural inclination to focus internally.

Michael Strong of FLOW knows he does his best thinking, reading, and writing early in the morning. As all three are essential to his work, he rarely schedules meetings or calls in the morning. He also knows that he is at his best one on one, and that he is most effective in meetings that focus on ideas rather than logistics. Knowing these characteristics, he tries to participate in long group meetings only if they are idea-focused, if his presence will add significant value, or if his colleagues specifically request that he attend.

While his job requires that he interact with groups of people all the time, John Mackey treasures his solitary time. In an effort to balance the intensity of his working life with his desire for time alone and with very close friends, John takes long-distance backpacking trips. These treks, often a month in length, allow him a much-needed respite from the very interactive business of running Whole Foods Market.

Our relationship to groups can inform how we design our office space and the size of our working teams. Do we use an open space plan or individual offices? To what extent are our teams self-managed? Do we engage our customers in an open dialogue about our products and services? The answers to these and other questions are informed by our relationship to groups, whether we are conscious of them or not.

SUMMARY: AWARENESS

We don't see things as they are, we see them as we are.

—ANAÏS NIN

As you may have noticed, cultivating awareness is not easy. In some respects the exercises for practicing awareness are simple and straightforward, but facing what comes up in the practice is often challenging, as we are called to look at aspects of ourselves we take for granted, do not care to see, or assume don't warrant our attention. To deeply cultivate awareness over time calls for curiosity, courage, and discipline. It is always humbling to deal with one's own mind.

Carrying awareness into work does not mean you become a pushover or are spaced out or ungrounded. On the contrary, deepening awareness and understanding of what is going on inside and around you prepares you to make clear, conscious decisions. It helps you see the motives, actions, and effects that others have on you and your business, and shows you how to address them thoughtfully, strategically, skillfully—and, when appropriate, ferociously.

The awareness practices introduced throughout this book provide a framework, along with many other such practices, for cultivating awareness. But awareness is not something we can predictably develop or achieve according to a formula. In most cases, ongoing cultivation and practice lead to ever-deepening awareness, but at times, when we go through particularly challenging passages, our awareness may not appear to be deepening. Awareness does not develop in a linear fashion. But fortunately, increasing awareness creates a virtuous spiral of increasing awareness and increasing ability to work with the challenges that arise when applying increased awareness. One of the principal benefits of awareness, then, is deepening awareness.

Writing Reflection: Awareness

The whole idea of awareness practice is to support you in being in the present moment and with the people who are in it with you, rather than ruminating about the past, projecting into the future, or otherwise being carried away by sensations, feelings, thoughts, and intuitions. We cultivate awareness so we can respond to challenges and opportunities rather than react to them, and we make conscious decisions that are informed by our inner experiences but not dictated by them.

Among the tools that support cultivating awareness are slowing down, observation, and curiosity. In this writing reflection, we will draw on many of the elements addressed in this chapter and exercise the various channels of perception to tune in to what success means to us. After all, since you are reading this book, you are undoubtedly seeking something, and you are actively involved as an entrepreneur or change agent, or intend to be. Whether you are looking for ideas, inspiration, meaning, guidance, or something else, you have some aspiration or intention to realize.

Have a pen and notebook handy. Take a few deep breaths and observe how you are seated. With each exhale, surrender your jaw and shoulders to gravity. With each inhale, feel your spine lengthen. Feel the two—the dropping jaw and shoulders and lifting spine—happening together.

Reflect on the following questions, and as you reflect on each, notice any sensations in your body, feelings or thoughts that might arise, intuitions that might pop up, any channel or channels you are drawn to—and, if you are inclined to do so, write about what you experience, and write your answer to the question.

Why are you reading this book? Breathe. Notice. Observe. Reflect. Respond. Breathe.

What do you hope to get out of this book? Breathe. Notice. Observe. Reflect. Respond. Breathe.

What do you hope to accomplish through your work? Breathe. Notice. Observe. Reflect. Respond. Breathe. What does success look like for you? Breathe. Notice. Observe. Reflect. Respond. Breathe.

What is your experience of yourself in relation to others in the context of your work? How do you envision working with others? Breathe. Notice. Observe. Reflect. Respond. Breathe.

How do you envision your business ecosystem functioning? What is the relationship between you and the stakeholders and between all of the stakeholders? Breathe. Notice. Observe. Reflect. Respond. Breathe.

Scan your body and notice any sensations. Scan your emotional body and notice any feelings. Notice any thoughts. Observe any insights or intuitions. What do you find?

If there is anything that is calling for your attention, follow it if you wish and write about your experience. If you have the time and interest, sit in silence for a few minutes, and just observe whatever comes up for you, through any channel; let it pass through or follow it with energy and attention, whichever feels right to you. Or switch off, back and forth: observing and letting the experiences pass through you, then choosing experiences to follow. In both cases, maintain your awareness of yourself and the process of observing and engaging.

This in itself is success—success that leads to success.

Chapter Three

EMBODIMENT

Vision without action is merely a dream.
Action without vision just passes the time.
Vision with action can change the world.

—ADAPTATION OF A TRADITIONAL JAPANESE SAYING

ran is an experienced software development strategist and engineer, specializing in children's educational software. Now in her mid-forties, she has worked throughout her career with easy-going, nonconfrontational artist/engineers who are tuned into children and their learning process. Due to changes in her industry, however, she has recently taken on a project in the highly competitive general education segment of the online publishing market. She finds a dramatically different culture in her new position and experiences big clashes between her own values and behaviors—which are inclusive, cooperative, and optimistic—and those of the people she works with. She feels pressured in this new environment to deliver new products with insufficient development timetables—a strategy she feels results in inferior quality.

Because she is nonconfrontational and comes from a vastly different corporate culture, Fran finds herself holding back from openly criticizing the product quality and the way people treat one another. This need to be inauthentic creates added stress. She often thinks of leaving the company, but has chosen to stay in hopes of finding the resolve—and skill—to have a positive impact on the company's products and culture. She recognizes that in order to do this, she needs to be assertive but not aggressive, nonjudgmental but constructively critical, and forthright but unattached to outcome.

To support her in developing these attributes and to achieve her objectives, Fran designs a research project to assess product quality and user perception. At the same time, she begins to study Aikido with a teacher who specifically applies the principles of this ancient Japanese martial art to collaborative problem-solving and nonviolent conflict resolution. Fran purposefully applies the lessons she is learning at the dojo in her dealings with her colleagues at work.

By standing up for her intentions and principles, making the commitment to make a difference, and finding ways to bring these literally into her body and into action, Fran feels empowered and enlivened, and knows that, even if the company and her colleagues do not shift, she has gained much and will have many other opportunities to make a difference through her work.

....

Embodiment: Applied awareness. The moving of thought into form, ideas into action.

....

While our awareness focuses inward—on our experience of ourselves, others, and groups—embodiment focuses outward: on how we carry our awareness into the world and through our work. If we use the metaphor of a mountain lake for awareness and our minds, then we will use the metaphor of a flowing river in its earthen riverbed for embodiment, with awareness as the river's source.

In this chapter, we will follow the course of the river of embodied awareness as it moves into our passion, intentions, and purpose, which become accelerating forces that, like gravity, propel us to the sea. Principles and commitments form the banks of the river and keep us from dissipating before we reach our destination, so we arrive whole and focused. We will apply the tools of awareness, through the multiple lenses of sensing, feeling, thinking, and intuiting. And we will reflect on the implications of our increasing embodiment for our relationships with ourselves, others, groups, and the integrated whole.

Moving Meditation Practice

Ultimately, embodiment means we carry our awareness practice into everyday life—sensing, observing, and releasing automatic reactions. We can apply it while walking or eating or doing almost anything. Mindfulness practice cultivated through movement draws on more of our capacity and creates a deeper fabric of awareness.

` With ongoing awareness practice, including movement and other multichannel practices, we can sustain and embody greater awareness in the most intense, challenging, highly charged, and fast-moving situations. We can also apply our practice of slowing down to heated situations, cooling the fire and creating clarity where speed and emotion may have blurred things.

While I have practiced mindfulness meditation for years, as well as various forms of yoga that include meditation practice, my current favorite awareness practices are moving meditations: ChiRunning and the 5Rhythms moving meditation practice. ChiRunning combines running with the biomechanics and awareness of Tai Chi. 5Rhythms systematically integrates movement, spatial relations, rhythmic patterns, introspection, recognition of the whole, and relating to others.

The next time you eat, take a walk, play golf, or engage in your favorite hobby, slow down and observe your inner experience—sensations, feelings, thoughts, and intuitions. And notice how the quality of your overall experience changes.

PASSION: WHAT TURNS YOU ON?

Follow your bliss!

—JOSEPH CAMPBELL

One of the things I enjoy most about my friends who are entrepreneurs and change agents is how passionate they are. Every conversation pulses with energy. And my favorites are the younger ones in their twenties and thirties who combine passion with the incredible energy and vitality of youth. Man, they are on fire! And fire catches.

Joseph Campbell, the late American mythologist who deeply understood people's dreams, aspirations, and manifestations, knew what he was talking about when he coined the phrase "Follow your bliss!" as key to fulfillment, happiness, and well-being. Passion may be the perpetual-motion machine that so many are looking for; it generates energy that generates more energy. Passion is the fire in the belly and the stirring in the heart that converts ideas into actions. Passion is the energy that fuels practice. It is the force that moves love into loving and caring into compassion.

Passion is contagious. It can also be seductive, even addictive. It feels good to be on fire, filled with energy and excitement. But there are risks, including burning out and burning out others. Passion calls for awareness to keep you from burning out or forcing others to flee.

I remember a powerful experience with an incredible person named Rick Little, president and chief executive officer of the ImagineNations Group, founder and former CEO of Quest International and the International Youth Foundation—organizations that help young people all over the world to find their path in life. At one point in our conversation, Rick asked me what I was passionate about. I responded that I was passionate about liberation and the expression of human potential, and supporting others to experience them for themselves. Rick then asked if I could see or feel a fire in my belly, and if so, to describe the fire. To my surprise, I saw hot glowing embers rather than a big, flaming, raging fire: the kind of embers you want to cook on, that last all night, and are still there in the morning burning steady and strong. It was a powerful moment, realizing that the wildfires of my youth had turned into a sustained and steady furnace. The image made great sense to me and persists to this moment.

In retrospect, it is not surprising that within six weeks of meeting Rick I attended my first FLOW retreat at John Mackey's ranch, and John and Michael asked me to serve as FLOW's executive director and chief activation officer (which requires some flames as well as hot coals). From that day on, my work has been explicitly focused on liberating the entrepreneurial spirit for good—pretty much a bull's-eye of the passion I expressed to Rick.

Since we tend to be passionate about things we are good at, passion and strength align easily. Passion draws us to our skills, and we are drawn to opportunities that turn us on and let us bring out talents to bear.

Exercise: What Turns You On?

Really, what turns you on? No holding back here. And pay attention to what comes up. Write it down. Reflect on it. Refine it. And go for it.

As you consider this question, tune in to your belly, right below your navel. Check it out. Breathe into it and feel it. What does it feel like? While you are observing the sensation, ask yourself the following questions, observing any changes in the sensations in your belly.

- What problems do you want to solve?
- What opportunities do you want to pursue?
- What activities make you come alive?
- If you could have any job you wanted or create any business or project you can imagine, what would it look like?

If one of the questions has more energy than the

others, answer it and reflect on your answer. Ask the question again. Get more specific if you can. And continue to ask the question until you feel you can go no further. Observe the sensation in your belly. How does it feel now?

Shift to an image of fire in your belly. What does the fire look like? What does it feel like? How does it make you feel? How does your answer to the original question make you feel? What turns you on?

Now go back to your belly and contemplate this question: What sustains your fire? As you answer it, feel your belly and its changing sensations. Find the factors that help your fire burn in a way that feels sustainable to you.

Take a few deep breaths. You can hold the feeling, or let it go. It will be there when you want to tap in to it.

INTENTIONS

You will become as small as your controlling desire, as great as your dominant aspiration.

—JAMES ALLEN

The ability to focus attention and energy on an objective and pursue its realization is one of our greatest capacities. If you have ever faced off against a two-year-old intent on getting something he or she desires, you know the innate power of human intention! Entrepreneurs, inventors, artists, and other creators have a similar power of intention.

Intentions reflect the yearnings of our being. They infuse our aspirations with energy, giving us targets to move toward while enlivening our movement. If our temperament influences our approach to things and passion gets us moving, then intentions orient us and draw us forward in a particular direction. When we pursue our passions with intention while leveraging and cultivating our strengths, magic happens. By focusing our attention and openly expressing our intentions, we make them conscious, explicit, and deliberate.

Exercise: What's Your Intention?

Find a comfortable position. Take a few deep breaths. With each inhale, feel your spine lengthen. With each exhale, feel your shoulders and jaw drop. Focus lightly—that is, don't hold on tightly—on your breath, watching the inhale and exhale. Observe whatever comes up—a sensation, a feeling, a thought, whatever; just observe it and let it pass. Come back to your breath. Slow. Easy. If you realize you've gotten carried away, just come back to your breath. Do this for as long as you like. This basic mindfulness meditation is good to practice anytime, for as long as you like. It is excellent mind-training. When you are ready, read on.

What intelligences do you intend to cultivate to apply to your work? How do you intend to cultivate them and apply them?

What is your passion? How do you intend to pursue

your passion in your work? How do you intend to apply your talents in pursuit of your passion?

Tune in to the fire in your belly. What does it feel like? What does it look like? As you breathe and sense the fire, tune in to your talents and your passion. What is happening with your fire? Is it changing in any way? Is it moving to other parts of your body?

When you are ready, take a few deep breaths and slowly come out of the exercise.

PURPOSE

This is the true joy in life—the being used for a purpose recognized by yourself as a mighty one; the being a force of nature instead of a feverish selfish clod of ailments and grievances complaining that the world will not devote itself to making you happy. I am of the opinion that my life belongs to the whole community, and as long as I live it is my privilege to do for it whatever I can. I want to be thoroughly used up when I die, for the harder I work, the more I live. I rejoice in life for its own sake. Life is no "brief candle" to me. It is sort of a splendid torch, which I have a hold of for the moment, and I want to make it burn as brightly as possible before handing it over to future generations.

—GEORGE BERNARD SHAW

Purpose is the essential, core, single underlying or overriding reason we move, as individuals and organizations. It is the big "why" underlying what we do.

On the most basic biological level, we may be driven to survive and reproduce, yet that is hardly the purpose of our existence. In the words of Ed Freeman, intellectual father of the stakeholder model of business management, "We need red blood cells to live (the same way a business needs profits to live), but the purpose of life is not to make red blood cells (the same way the purpose of business is not to exist to make profits)."

Purpose is an activating, motivating, and animating force. It is what moves us to get up in the morning to dive into life with our full being. Purpose sustains us when times get tough, and serves as a guiding star when we stray off course. An assistant's purpose may be to provide administrative services that allow his colleagues to succeed; a teacher's purpose may be to create nurturing environments for children to learn and grow; an inventor's purpose might be to bring innovative products to life that help people overcome pain. Whatever our circumstances, knowing our purpose has the effect of focusing our business's products, services, and processes toward goals larger than just making money.

Purposeful people build purposeful companies. And purposeful people make an impact through whatever their work or role may be. Purpose at work, in business or otherwise, has two dimensions: the purpose of the individuals making up the organization, and the purpose of the organization itself.

Building from the foundation of awareness—and specifically, awareness of our tendencies, passions, and intentions—we can identify and deeply align with our purpose, a key step in activating our ability to make a difference while flourishing.

Purpose is a powerful force, a perennial theme addressed by philosophers, and a major focus of business leaders, researchers, consultants, and others looking at the keys to catalyzing conscious businesses with inspired team members, engaged customers, and other stakeholders working in unison. Purpose is one of the three principal tenets of the definition of Conscious Capitalism espoused by John Mackey and FLOW. The authors of *Firms of Endearment* identify purpose as one of the keys to success of the "FoEs." Jim Collins, author of the bestselling *Built to Last* and *Good to Great*, defines purpose as a company's fundamental reason for being—its soul. In *It's Not What You Sell, It's What You Stand For*, Roy Spence Jr. and Haley Rushing tell great stories of the power of purpose in the success of clients like Southwest Airlines (to democratize the airways: "Freedom to Fly"), Wal-Mart (to save people money so they can live better: "Save Money, Live Better"), and BMW (to enable people to experience the joy of driving: "Sheer Driving Pleasure"). Great companies with the most significant impact and influence invariably have clear and compelling purposes—like the Walt Disney Company, dedicated to making people happy, and Mary Kay Cosmetics, created to give unlimited opportunity to women.

And the idea of purpose is not limited to business. Reflecting the mass attraction of purpose, Rick Warren's *The Purpose Driven Life* is the bestselling nonfiction hardcover book ever, selling more than twenty million copies.

At the Catalyzing Conscious Capitalism event which FLOW coproduced in the fall of 2008, Sally Jewel, CEO of REI, told the story of how REI refined its understanding of its purpose through a process of repeatedly asking the question "Why?" Bestselling business author Jim Collins writes about the same process as the "Five Whys." Roy Spence Jr. and Haley Rushing also outline this process in their book along with other tools to facilitate the inquiry. We can apply the process of asking "Why?" to discover and refine our individual purpose and that of our organizations.

In its simplest form, we begin with the question: What do we do? As in, what is our business organized to do? What things do we make, or what services do we deliver? For whom? The next question: Why do we do that? The next question: Why do we do that? The next question: Why do we do that? And again: Why do we do that? As we analyze the answers to each of these "whys," a picture of our purpose emerges. In the case of REI, the company discovered that its purpose is to inspire, educate, and outfit for a lifetime of outdoor adventure.

Here's an example of how the process can work. Let's use Sue the Idealist as our example. Her project is called YEP!: Youth Empowerment Project. Here is her process:

- *What do we intend to do through YEP!?* We provide training in leadership, self-care, personal mastery, and team building for inner-city youth.
- *Why do we do that?* We believe that these skills are essential for success in life, and that the inner-city communities and cultures do not provide this education. So we are filling in a gap.
- *Why do we do that?* We are filling in this gap because we believe that human potential is the greatest resource on the planet, and that wasting it is a crime against nature. And we believe that all of humanity will be served if we can elevate the most disenfranchised with the greatest potential, by teaching them to elevate themselves.
- *Why do we do that?* We focus on teaching the most disenfranchised with the greatest potential because their success serves as an inspiration to others and they become leaders within their own communities, committed to supporting others to have a similar experience of

empowerment to their own. This builds the spiritual foundation of the community and creates a positive culture.

- *Why do we do that?* We focus on building conscious community and a culture of opportunity because it becomes generative and self-sustaining.
- *The YEP! purpose:* To create a conscious community and culture of opportunity that supports young people to develop the skills, mind-set, and network of support to find their passion and purpose, and to pursue their dreams with confidence, skill, and success.

Jack, the tech entrepreneur, may have come up with a purpose that reads "InsightWidgit exists to support Web users with instant access to timeless wisdom to inform their travels through the Web and through their lives." The green tech company where Evan, the project manager, works, might have a purpose such as: "To create products and services that enhance life for people everywhere, while reducing the impact of their consumption on the planet." And Jocelyn the artist might have as her purpose, "To open people to the possibility that they can make a positive difference in the world through their thoughts and actions and to inspire them to change what they think and do."

Let's try it ourselves.

Exercise: Finding Our Why

You can apply this exercise to define your personal purpose, or the purpose of your business, or both. You can replace the "I" in the questions below with "we" if you want to focus on the purpose of your business rather than on your personal one.

Once again, begin by tuning in to your awareness instrument—yourself! Have your reflections on your passion and intentions handy, or in mind, for this exercise. And I encourage you to write down your responses to the questions below.

Find a comfortable position. Take a few deep breaths. With each inhale, feel your spine lengthen. With each exhale, feel your shoulders and jaw drop.

Tune in to your body as you reflect on your passion and intentions. Or as you reconsider these questions: What is your passion? What are your intentions?

Now reflect on this question and write down your response to it: What do I do? Spend some time with it. Describe what you do in some detail, including whom you do it for.

Now address this question: Why do I do that?

And in reflecting on your response, answer it again: Why do I do that?

And again: Why do I do that?

One more time: Why do I do that?

Now look back at all of your responses and find the pieces that fit together to describe your core purpose. Once you have done this, take more time to distill it down to the shortest statement that captures the essence of your purpose. This is the most challenging step. As Mark Twain said, "I would have written a shorter letter, if I had more time."

Take a moment to reflect on your temperament, passion, intentions, and purpose, and observe how they line up. You may want to scan your body to see how it responds to your draft purpose statement. Or scan your emotions, thoughts, and intuition.

Take a few deep breaths. And proceed on.

I highly recommend Roy Spence Jr. and Haley Rushing's book, *It's Not What You Sell, It's What You Stand For*, as a practical guide for defining your purpose, filled with inspiring examples.

PRINCIPLES

In matters of style, swim with the current; in matters of principle, stand like a rock.

—THOMAS JEFFERSON

Infused with purpose and passion as we move with energy and direction, principles are the values, universal truths, and moral and ethical aspirations and standards inspiring and guiding our behavior. They provide grounding and direction. They represent what we stand for and what we are willing to stand up for. They support us in maintaining alignment with our intentions and purpose. Principles structure our behavior, ensuring that we respect others and the world around us and that our purpose and passion do not overflow the banks and create unintended, unconscious damage.

Consider the implications of conducting ourselves in business based on principles such as:

- Not compromising quality for cost
- Not jeopardizing friendships through our business decisions
- Resolving conflicts through open dialogue, facilitated if necessary
- Making major business decisions with consideration for the implications for people, planet, and profit

Such principles are essential to Working for Good. They inform strategies, tactics, plans, and practices, and form the underlying ethos of an organization or enterprise. Principles establish priorities and define our bottom line. They provide light to guide the way through challenges and into opportunities. When principles guide our behavior and animate our work, process and product are aligned, and ends and means are essentially one. Principles help us answer the questions: "What is the right thing to do under these circumstances?" and "How do we respond to this?"

If principles guide our behavior, and the intention of our behavior is to engage and inspire others to bring their time, energy, passion, commitment, creativity, hearts, and souls to create something incredible together, then our principles must cultivate trust, respect, loyalty, care, enthusiasm, initiative, and responsibility.

Principle: Servant Leadership

When the Master governs, the people
are hardly aware that he exists. …
The Master doesn't talk, he acts.
When his work is done,
the people say "Amazing:
we did it, all by ourselves!"

—LAO TZU, *Tao Te Ching*

If our ultimate intention is to manifest higher purpose, cultivate presence, inspire mastery, and embody love, then servant leadership is the path to success. And if our process of Working for Good includes personal and collective growth and development, then servant leadership is a natural, universal principle to guide our decisions and behavior.

The term "servant leadership," first coined in 1970 by Robert K. Greenleaf in an essay entitled "The Servant as Leader," reflects the practices of spiritual masters and inspirational leaders throughout human history. By focusing on the needs of others and working to address them, the servant leader engenders deep trust, confidence, and loyalty and models behaviors that foster collaboration and mitigate conflict.

The idea of the servant leader stretches far back into human history, as many of the great leaders and spiritual masters—including Jesus, the Buddha, and others from whom emerged great faiths—embodied characteristics attributable to servant leaders today.

The servant leader is first a servant, motivated by the drive to serve. Through the act of serving, the aspiration to lead emerges naturally. The nature and expression of this leadership is dramatically different from leadership generated from the desire to lead.

The rewards for leading through service are profound, including deep personal growth and strength, the joy of witnessing others flourish, and the confidence that comes from the trust, engagement, commitment, energy, and more that servant leadership evokes from others.

We can define and employ principles to guide our behavior in general, our relationships with others, the way we come together in groups, and the way we relate as a whole system. In addition to the principle of servant leadership outlined above, two other principles are gaining significant prominence: transparency and authenticity.

Transparency is the rule in the wired and wireless world, where billions of people have immediate access to nearly infinite information. Through the blogosphere and videosphere, one person's experience with a product, service, or company can become common knowledge overnight. The previously secret art and science of product development is now increasingly done in the open marketplace by openly engaging outsiders and even customers. eBay has built the Web's premier commerce site based on the transparency of transactions and on its reputation rating system. Similarly, the performance ratings of third-party sellers through Amazon.com are visible to all.

Authenticity is not something we can embody at will. Rather, it is something to aspire to and align with. As a principle, it provides a benchmark for our behavior. If our actions line up with our intentions, purpose, and principles, we are authentic. If they do not, then we are not.

Authenticity is a lot like presence; you can feel it when it is there and you can feel its absence when it is not there. Authenticity builds trust, which builds relationships. When we feel that a person or a company is authentic, we can settle into our relationship with confidence that they will deliver what they promise and stand behind whatever they deliver. And we will often trust them enough to take risks with them, including buying new products and services from them, or following their lead into new territory.

Exercise: Identifying Principles

Stand comfortably, with your knees slightly bent. Take a few deep breaths. With each inhale, feel your spine lengthen. With each exhale, feel your shoulders and jaw drop. Feel the soles of your feet on the ground and the weight of your body resting on your feet. Feel solid on the ground.

Breathe into your chest. Feel your chest rise and fall with your breath. If you can, feel your heart center opening or warming as you breathe. And continue to feel your feet on the ground and your weight heavy on your feet. Breathe and sink. Breathe and open your heart.

Contemplate and complete the following lines (you can write your reflections when you are done with the exercise).

I stand for _____, _____, and _____.

I value _____ and _____,
and I act in accordance with these values.

My bottom line is _____. I will
not compromise this value.

You can play with these lines. Answer them multiple
times in various ways. When you are done, you can
write your responses and reflect.

COMMITMENTS

*Until one is committed, there is hesitancy, the chance to draw
back, always ineffectiveness. Concerning all acts of initiative
(and creation), there is one elementary truth the ignorance
of which kills countless ideas and splendid plans: that the
moment one definitely commits oneself, then providence moves
too. A whole stream of events issues from the decision, raising
in one's favor all manner of unforeseen incidents, meetings,
and material assistance, which no man could have dreamt
would have come his way.*

*Whatever you can do, or dream you can, begin it.
Boldness has genius, power, and magic in it. Begin it now!*

—JOHANN WOLFGANG VON GOETHE

When we commit, things happen. Intention and purpose
establish our direction and focus our attention. Principles
ensure that the ground beneath us is solid. Commitment
takes us to the point of no return, or to the point where
there are consequences to pay if we try to return. Part

of the power of expressing commitment to others is that we establish a bond: a responsibility to act or to communicate our reasons for inaction. Intention establishes our aspirations and vision of the future; purpose constitutes our core reason for being. Principles set the parameters of our actions. Commitment brings our intention, purpose, and principles to life.

Commitment is essential for any process of discovery and creation. Every entrepreneur I know has a creation story and stories about passages in the evolution of their businesses. These tales begin with their commitment, and to their wonder and surprise they unfold almost magically, even if the path is challenging and painful. Making a commitment is like setting out onto a big river in a small but sufficient boat. Somehow we know we are not going to sink, but we also know we are called to stay awake. To some extent, we can guide or steer the boat, and to some extent, the river has a mind of its own and reveals the journey as we wind around each curve and pass through each set of rapids.

Keeping commitments is one of the most powerful building blocks of integrity—the ability to congruently hold together, the way a tree holds together with its roots seamlessly connected to its trunk, which seamlessly connects to its branches and out to its leaves. If our intention aligns with our expression, which aligns with our actions, we cultivate integrity—and others recognize us for it.

Keeping our word to ourselves is the initial step in keeping our commitments. Keeping our word to others ensues from there. Holding each other accountable for our commitments is a great service we provide to one another. A short list of core commitments for Working for Good might include: continually cultivate awareness, stay on purpose, act according to principles, and support one another in doing all three of these.

Exercise: Establishing Commitments

Reflect on and respond to the following questions:

What commitments do you make with respect to your intentions and principles?

- How will you monitor your words and actions?
- How will you respond when you find you are contradicting your intentions and principles?

What commitments do you make with respect to yourself?

- Will you allow yourself the time to check in with yourself?
- How will you take care of yourself?
- Will you develop a supportive environment and network for yourself?

What commitments do you make with respect to your relations to and interactions with your team members?

- How will you communicate with each other?
- What supportive patterns and practices will you develop and apply?
- How will you hold each other accountable to your commitments?

What commitments do you make with respect to your relations to and interactions with customers?

- Will the customer always be right, or will there be limits to your customers' power over your business and the way you conduct it?
- Will the customer be respected as an integral aspect of your business with an important role to play in its development over time?
- How will you communicate to and support customers in their interactions with your business and its products and services?

What commitments do you make to other stakeholder groups? To vendors? To investors? To the community? To the environment?

Process Work: Moving into Connection with Awareness

While embodied awareness is a gateway to connection, and mindfulness lays the ground for the skills of connection, I want to introduce one more tool to foster embodied awareness and bring awareness to life. The tool is called Process Work, a discipline developed by Arny Mindell that integrates Jungian psychology, physics, and Taoism, among other philosophies and systems.

In mindfulness practice, we observe what we are experiencing through the channel along which we are experiencing it, without judgment and with open acceptance, until it passes through and gives way to another perceived experience—whether it be a sensation, feeling, thought, or intuition. The practice of Process Work builds on this detached observation of experience and engages with our awareness—with what we are observing and experiencing. While mindfulness observes, Process Work engages.

In Process Work, we observe signals in the dreambody (the composite of psyche and soma as they relate to each other in an integrated whole) through its various channels, amplify them and follow them as they unfold, and often switch to other channels until underlying meaning is revealed. Bodily processes, like physical pains and symptoms, emotions, habitual patterns of movement, and social behaviors, hold deeper meaning, which we can reveal by working with them. Here's an example:

Many years ago, when visiting with a young friend who was experiencing a profound transition in his work, I supported him in discovering his next steps by facilitating a process. Robert, as we will call him, was the youngest in his family—a family that had built a substantial business over many decades, with many divisions and product lines. All of his siblings were executives in the business, and he was torn between joining the business at a low level, finding a place for himself where he could assume significant responsibility, or pursuing a different path altogether as an artist. He is an understated and private person, yet passionate about many things and very much engaged in the world.

When I asked him if I could pose questions about his relationship to the business, his family, and his art to see if we might find some insights to support his decision, he agreed. I listened carefully to his responses and his tone of voice, and I watched his body position and movements. At one point, when I was inquiring into his relationship with his family and how it influenced his decision, I noted that, while his voice was even and he didn't have much to say, his arm was making a strong, distinct motion up and down with his elbow bending and straightening and his finger pointing as he spoke. I asked him to exaggerate the motion and follow it as long as it had energy. His hand and arm motion became more and more intense. I asked him if there was a sound that went with the motion, and he immediately started grunting loudly, continuing to move his arm up and down as the grunting grew louder. Finally, I asked him if there was a message, if there was something he wanted to say, something his arm movement and grunting were trying to express. The grunting shifted into a chorus of "I can do it! I can do it! I can do it!"

After a while the energy subsided and Robert came back to a normal, resting state. When I asked him what it all meant to him, he told me he had felt insecure about expressing to his family his strong feelings about taking over the leadership of the family foundation, and for months had not been able to muster the confidence. This led him to waver in his overall decision about what to do next, and kept him in a somewhat suspended state. Soon thereafter, he met with his family, expressed his feelings and intentions, and quickly became president of the family foundation, a position he held for many years with great success for himself and the foundation. He became a source of pride for his family.

In mindfulness practice, we observe and let go. In Process Work, we observe, engage with, and move into what we observe. Both practices are powerful tools we can apply to our work as entrepreneurs and change agents to facilitate increased personal and collective awareness.

Mindfulness is not easy. As you know if you practice mindfulness meditation (or as you will learn as you do so), being present to sensations, feelings, thoughts, and insights, yet not identifying with them—that is, realizing you are not what you sense, feel, think, or know—is no easy thing. Your ability to be mindful varies with internal conditions and external circumstances. Process Work, or process meditation, adds a layer of complexity as we combine nonidentified observation with engagement, moving with what we are observing rather than simply observing it. Let's try it now, beginning with mindfulness. You will note that we've already done this in some of the exercises in the last chapter, moving from sensations to feelings and from sensations and feelings into thoughts.

Exercise: Following a Process

Read or listen to the following. Don't worry about your starting position; you can draw on anything you observe, even if it is a tight jaw, hunched shoulders, a slouching spine, or an uncomfortable seat!

Pick a channel, any channel. Or just start observing yourself and see what comes up—a sensation, feeling, thought, or intuition. Observe whatever emerges. If you find it interesting, or if it has energy for you, stay with it. If not, move on. When you find something that interests you or has energy around it—a strong sensation, an intense feeling, a relentless thought, or a captivating insight—go into it. Explore it. Focus on the intensity and see if you can make it more intense. What is it saying to you? If it has an answer, uncover it; if it wants to lead you to another experience (in the same channel or another one) go for it, but see if you can sustain the intensity. If it starts to wane, see if you can amplify it. Continue until you feel some sense of resolution, or until you cannot sustain it any longer.

How was that for you? To what extent could you sustain the intensity and follow the experience? What, if anything, did it reveal to you?

You can try this again, beginning with a specific question you want to answer or issue you want to address, and see what signals come up as you contemplate your question or issue.

Mindfulness is a profoundly useful tool. Over time it increases our ability to remain present in the face of strong distractions and intense challenges. Process meditation makes awareness more interactive, supporting us to move with awareness and produce results with great energy, focus, and speed.

SUMMARY: EMBODIMENT

We who lived in concentration camps can remember the men who walked through the huts comforting others, giving away their last piece of bread. They may have been few in number, but they offer sufficient proof that everything can be taken away from a man but one thing: the last of the human freedoms—to choose one's attitude in any given set of circumstances, to choose one's own way.

—VIKTOR FRANKL

The awareness practices I introduced in Chapter Two support us to identify our passion, intentions, purpose, principles, and commitments, monitor how we are embodying them, and get us back on track when we are off course. Practicing awareness and being aligned with our intentions, purpose, and principles helps us make clear, conscious decisions and to walk the edges with the recognition that we are doing so.

When we face the question "What do I do when I can go this way, or that?" we can tune in to our awareness, tap into the wisdom of our mind-body, weigh our decisions against our intentions, purpose, and principles, and move forward from a place of integrity.

An employer named Henry went through seven years of hell at the hands of an agency of the U.S. government after he was falsely accused by a malicious employee trying to cover himself. When his case finally went to court—after hundreds of thousands of dollars, harassment at the hands of prosecutors, and a complete disruption of his business and life—the case against him was so lame (the three witnesses called to testify against him all testified in his defense, acknowledging his honesty and integrity) that he won without putting up a defense. And the accuser turned out to have a history of leaving marriages, dishonorable discharge from the military, and drug abuse. When it was all over, Henry reflected, "You think you have it all, and somebody takes it all away from you, with no justice. Then you see all the people who have no power, who deserve it as much as we do."

Henry's core strength is service with integrity. His passion, intention, purpose, principles, and commitment all align to serve and care for others. Out of his ordeal, he created a company designed to empower people to take control of their medical care through a win-win process for all stakeholders. It has become a growing community of dedicated, inspired collaborators, passionately sharing his purpose.

When life serves us lemons, we have the opportunity to make lemonade. And when life gives us the opportunity to discover and embrace our purpose and pursue its conscious manifestation, we embark on a remarkable journey of unfolding experience, growth, and development.

The four characters we met earlier will each have a different way of approaching the elements of embodiment. Jack the Rational is passionate about applying the latest scientific developments to new products. His intention is to make the world a better place through innovation. His purpose is to bring ideas to life. His principles focus on fostering excellence and accomplishment. Jocelyn the Artisan is passionate about communicating through art and changing the way people view the world based on novel sensory experiences. Her intention and purpose are to create these experiences. Her principles relate to freedom, self-expression, and bringing ideas into action. Sue the Idealist is passionate about personal growth and pursuing idealistic vision. Her intention is to serve others and make the world a better place through her work. Her purpose is to empower youth. Her principles and commitments are based on relationships. Evan the Guardian is passionate about order and peace. His intention is to do what he can to ensure that order and peace are sustained and propagated. His purpose is to bring order and peace to whatever he does. His principles and commitments are based on fostering clear, consistent relationships and processes.

It is important to recognize that our intelligence profile—the ways we learn and relate to the world—and temperament significantly influence and inform our passion, intentions, purpose, principles, and commitments. Awareness practice can help us to tune in to our tendencies and recognize how we align ourselves with them in setting our direction and making decisions.

In this chapter, we explored the flow of embodiment emerging from awareness, moving through passion, intentions, purpose, principles, and commitments. Along the way, we explored how we move in relation to our awareness and the elements within us that manifest through our actions. In the next chapter, we venture into the space where our river of embodied awareness merges with others who may have different levels of awareness and embodiment, as well as different worldviews, passions, intentions, purposes, principles, and commitments. We will explore the effect we have on others, their response to us, and the process of connecting—to foster shared awareness, passion, intentions, purpose, principles, and commitments, and embody them together.

One of the key measures of embodiment is presence: a state of being present that others can feel. If you put people first (another good principle) and really show up for them with an open heart and mind, they are more likely to be open, flexible, respectful, and present in return.

Presence is a by-product of pursuing our purpose with passion, fulfilling our commitments in alignment with principles, and cultivating embodied awareness. While presence is not something we can conjure up on demand, it is something we can evoke through the act of consistently being present. Presence is a powerful attracting force, activating and sustaining connection.

Writing Reflection: Embodiment

Have paper and pen handy, sit comfortably, and after tuning in through whatever means you like—breathing, scanning, etc.—draw from your reflections on your passion, intentions, purpose, principles, and commitments and draft a job description for yourself, beginning or finishing with a title that captures the spirit of your essential role. As you will recall, my title is chief activation officer, which reflects my intention and commitment to get things going: this seems to be my purpose as well as my passion.

As you do this exercise, you may want to meditate on each element—i.e., strength, passion, etc. You may want to check in with your sensations, emotions, thoughts, and intuitions. Whatever feels right to you.

When you are done, stand up again. Feel your feet on the ground and your weight resting on your feet and read your statement, feeling it in your body. Imagine yourself moving through your days embodying this role. How does it feel?

Chapter Four

CONNECTION

*Do not depend on the hope of results. You may have to face
the fact that your work will be apparently worthless and even
achieve no result at all, if not perhaps results opposite to what
you expect. As you get used to this idea, you start more and more
to concentrate not on the results, but on the value, the rightness,
the truth of the work itself. You gradually struggle less and less
for an idea and more and more for specific people. In the end,
it is the reality of personal relationship that saves everything.*

—THOMAS MERTON

S anjev is a marketing expert in the green/sustain-
ability field, who has had as his clients many highly
admired green and socially responsible companies. He
is respected for his creative strategies and effective campaigns,
but he has a reputation for being excessively focused on his
ideas and objectives, uninterested in what others think or
have to contribute, and, consequently, for being a terrible listener. He succeeded in the past based on his brilliance, charm,
and lack of real competition. But little by little, business

started drying up and he saw a slowdown in new business. Miriam, a close friend and ally, took the risk of telling him that he had a reputation "out on the street" for being self-absorbed and argumentative. He initially told her that it was other people's fault, not his. Anyone who complained about him either didn't see his genius or were threatened by it. But over time, he started to open to the idea that perhaps he had something to do with the situation. At that point, Miriam recommended that he talk with my colleague Elad Levinson for coaching.

Assessing Sanjev's Myers-Briggs personality profile in conjunction with feedback from close colleagues, as well as from his wife and oldest daughter, Elad could see clear patterns in his behavior. When others are listening to him, Sanjev is animated, charming, and engaging, but when they are talking, he is distant, distracted, and disconnected. Elad suggested that he needs to learn how to balance his genius with the ability to be receptive, quiet, and interested in others' perceptions. To this end, he gave Sanjev an assignment: visit with Miriam and do three things.

First, arrive with curiosity—specifically, bring a list of questions to ask her about her and her work. Second, ask questions *three times more often* than tell her what he is thinking. Third, be reflective. Instead of responding immediately, take a moment to really consider what Miriam is saying and be truly open to trying out new behavior.

The initial experiment was a success, and Sanjev began employing this approach to new business presentations. He would begin with questions, reflect on the answers, and incorporate the information into his responses. While Sanjev acknowledged that he felt somewhat mechanical in the process, since it did not come naturally to him, he also noticed that he received a very different response from his clients—and had more projects in the pipeline. He also noticed that his oldest daughter was suddenly spending more time with him, even asking him to do things with her, which she hadn't done in years.

Connection: A state in which two or more people engage in active relationship.
The act or process of cultivating and sustaining such a relationship.

Sanjev's story reflects the essence of connection. Connection is about letting go of our story and our agenda, meeting the other person as a whole person rather than as an object we want to move in one way or another. Like the tortoise and the hare, moving fast does not always get us to the finish line first. This is especially true when it comes to relationships with others. Clearly, awareness is the first step in opening space for connection—first we must recognize that we are filling the space with our stories and agendas. The next step is letting them go. In the context of business, with the complex dynamics and often overwhelming exigencies of the daily adventure, we need to check in with ourselves often. Ideally, we should have agreements, procedures, and systems in place to ensure that we check in with one another, too, and hold one another to our commitments to practice mindful awareness and cultivate connection.

As we move our passion and purpose into the sphere of relationships, we must engage with others to manifest our intentions and fulfill our commitments. If we want to do so with ease, grace, and flow—and flourish in the process—we have to connect consciously. In the realm of embodiment, our inclination is to employ awareness to *understand* our temperament, talent, and tendencies, but not try to transcend them. In the realm of connection—to the extent that any of these limit our ability to connect with other aspects of ourselves and with others—we *do* seek to transcend them.

Exercise: Tuning In to Connection

Take a few breaths. Feel your body. Move a little bit. Anything up for you? Observe it until it passes (unless you need to deal with it) and then read on.

Imagine you are making a business call to an important client or colleague. Her assistant answers the phone. How do you greet him? What is your experience of him? Do a quick body scan or an emotional body scan or a scan of your thoughts. What do you find? What do you say to this person? How do you relate to him?

Now imagine you are talking with the client or colleague you called. How do you greet her? What is your experience of her? Do a quick body scan or an emotional body scan or a scan of your thoughts. What do you find? How do you relate to her?

Are there differences between the way you greeted and related to the assistant and the person you called to talk with?

Now imagine you are on the phone with someone else, having an uncomfortable or superficial conversation. When you say goodbye before hanging up the phone, what is your last thought? How does that last instant feel to you? Do you recognize any body sensations that accompany that last instant on the phone? Describe them.

Okay, now take a couple of deep breaths and shake the experience off.

George Morgan was a professor of applied mathematics who, in the early seventies, went back to Harvard to study humanities. When he returned to Brown, instead of teaching applied mathematics, he taught a series of extra-departmental "university courses" called "Conceptions of Man," "Between Man and Man," and "Possibilities for Social Reconstruction," the last of which I took during the first semester of my senior year. It was by far the most engaging and inspiring class I took during my four years at Brown, with reverberations that continue to inform me.

The small, intimate class convened twice weekly in a circle. After opening the semester reading and discussing three books—*I and Thou* by Martin Buber, *Tools for Conviviality* by Ivan Illich, and *The Pentagon of Power* by Lewis Mumford—pairs of students prepared curricula for the rest of the semester and each week presented a topic to the group, which became the focus of the group's dialogue that week. George established a "container" for dialogue based on mutual respect, deep listening, and thoughtful inquiry. The experience of "Possibilities for Social Reconstruction" and the shared understanding that emerged through dialogue, in the context of a safe container cultivated through conscious process, represents a model for connection, as we will explore in this chapter.

To continue with our clear mountain lake metaphor for awareness and our river metaphor for embodiment, we can look at connection as the merging of two or more rivers. Taking George Morgan's lead, we'll begin with the concept of "I and Thou" to establish a safe container, or a strong and stable riverbed, in which to hold this convergence. Then we'll explore and honor the creative chaos, a concept George embraced, that happens when two or more beings with their respective views and energies come together. From there we'll move through some of the elements and issues we can work with to establish and deepen connection.

I AND THOU

When two people relate to each other authentically and humanly, God is the electricity that surges between them.

—MARTIN BUBER

There are two essential ways of relating to ourselves and others: as "I" or "it," a subject or an object. According to the philosophy of Martin Buber, we only become an "I" when we engage with others as "You" or "Thou" rather than as "it"—objects. Consider the manager who treats employees like pawns on a chessboard or cogs in a machine, versus one who expresses care and concern for them, who shows genuine interest in their families and lends support when needed. The difference is palpable. To be fully human is to be connected with another in conscious presence.

When we engage ourselves with awareness and treat others as whole beings who are no different from and no less than ourselves, magic happens. The electricity Buber speaks about is palpable and sets the conditions for sustainable connection.

This experience of connecting deeply with another person and becoming fully ourselves as we fully acknowledge the other, is one of those things we know the truth of based on our experience of it. We can talk about it all we want, but it is through the *being in* experience that it makes sense. It transcends our individual way of relating to the world, our personality type, even our language and culture.

Exercise: I and Thou

As you might expect, this exercise requires two people. So, if you would like to practice it, find a partner. Its purpose is to experience and cultivate mindful presence with another person.

Sit comfortably facing each other—close enough that you can touch each other's knee if you try to, but not so close that you feel uncomfortably "in each other's face."

Take a few deep breaths. With each inhale, feel your spine lengthen. With each exhale, feel your shoulders and jaw drop.

You can lightly hold hands or put your hands on each

other's knees—or not (whatever you both feel comfortable doing).

Now look into the other person's left eye, the window into their right brain. Sustain your attention there. Breathe, and simply observe any sensations, feelings, or thoughts that arise.

Continue for a few minutes, then relax. You can reflect on the experience and discuss it with the other person. How was it different from your normal contact with people? What did it feel like to be with another person and not follow your sensations, feelings, and thoughts?

In Buddhist cosmology, greed (or grasping), aversion (which includes fear), and delusion are the three root causes or sources of attitudes and behaviors that lead to suffering. These factors lead us to hold on to a particular view or position and create stories about what others are thinking or doing that lead to separation rather than connection.

Greed says: "They have what I want, or I need to hold on to what I have, whether it is wealth, a position, power, influence, or opportunity." Aversion or fear thinks: "They are trying to take something away from me, to hurt me, to diminish me. I despise and fear them." Delusion muses: "I'm not sure what is right or wrong, and rather than risk making a mistake, I am going to sustain confusion and chaos. I'm not sure how I feel about them. I kind of like them, but I'm not sure it is safe to trust them. Best to be nice to them but avoid them when I can."

It is hard to admit when we are ruled by any of these forces, or a dynamic combination of them, but it happens all the time. When fear steps in, we may tighten up and become impatient and short-tempered with others. When greed colors our perception, we may act in our narrow self-interest without concern for others, even if reciprocity serves all. And when we are operating under delusion, we are disconnected from a shared reality. Unless we release ourselves from their grasp, we cannot truly open to one another, because these forces's voices will always come between us, color our perceptions, and inhibit us from true openness to the other. Connection requires that we transcend their grip; awareness practice is our liberator.

BEYOND OUR CONTROL

One must still have chaos in oneself to be able to give birth to a dancing star.

—FRIEDRICH NIETZSCHE

While our intention may be to connect and we may cultivate the presence to show up as "I" and meet the other as "Thou," the process of connecting is not automatic and typically not without bumps and challenges. After all, we each bring the whole story of our lives with us, including our baggage from the past and the stresses of the present.

If we think about two rivers converging into one, there is always turbulence where the two meet, as their respective forces bang into each other. Before hot and cold blend to make warm, they wrestle with each other. Oil and vinegar require vigorous shaking to become vinaigrette. Without the shaking, they remain separate. In his inspiring book *The*

Silent Pulse, George Leonard tells the story of how tribes of Yanomami Indians in the Venezuelan Amazon come together. The chiefs of the two tribes go out into the jungle and, standing face to face, nearly nose to nose, yell at each other, back and forth, for a long time, with their bodies forcefully mirroring the energy of their yelling. They continue this way until eventually the yelling and body movement slow down into a connected, fluid, dancelike flow, referred to as rhythmic entrainment. Then they return to the village and the two tribes join in celebration.

While not every chaotic commencement is as dramatic as that of the Yanomami, and not every one leads to convergence, the potential for connection is always present. Our challenge and opportunity are to transcend our doubt and fear and overcome the blocks in our awareness—to find the path to connection, which, as reflected in the examples I have just offered, is often counterintuitive and can require that we move more deeply into the chaos in search of the calm eye at the center of the storm.

Exercise: Beyond Our Control

While we might aspire to control, control is an illusion. Let's try to control something simple. How about our thoughts?

Get into a comfortable position and take a few breaths. Relax your jaw and shoulders. Elevate your spine. And breathe.

Now pay attention to your thoughts; watch as thoughts appear. Now tell yourself to stop thinking.

No more thoughts; just watch what happens. Keep breathing and stop your thinking. How's it going?

Quite frankly, stopping your thoughts is essentially impossible—unless, perhaps, you spend all day every day for a long time doing nothing but meditating and training your mind to slow down to the point of not generating thoughts.

Now imagine you are sitting with someone else—or actually do so. Ask him or her to stop thinking. How successful do you think you will be with that instruction?

Now try it with a whole group. Any luck?

You may as well try to control the weather. Or evolution. Or your own aging process.

You get the point. Whether on a small or large scale, there is essentially very little we can actually control.

Most of us, especially in business, fear chaos. We like things to be predictable and well-ordered: under control. I can remember how unsettling it was for me when I first faced a colleague's tears. Tears in general were challenging to me, and I found this frightening for quite a while. But over time, as I opened to the sheer chaos and unfettered expression of emotion in tears, I learned the power of sharing the journey and participating in the process of resolution. I have learned that tears clear unexpressed emotion and bottled-up stress and lead to a beautiful resolution, which often brings great insights and clarity as well as peace. I find that the more quickly and fully I can engage with tears, my own or those of others, without resistance or interference, the quicker and more graceful the resolution.

I find the same general pattern to be true in business, or any other aspect of life. If I don't resist the chaos—instead recognize, embrace, and enter into it without resistance—resolution reveals itself. And to a meaningful extent, we can establish conditions to consciously work with chaos and conflict by cultivating a container of awareness, shared understanding, and safe process. If we are going to bring the best we have to offer to our work, we need to be our full selves and find ways to work with and through the stages and states that capture us as we engage in our journey together.

We don't have to process everything directly in the context of our work (we can draw on outside resources and support groups) but we can recognize that we all go through existential, emotional, and other challenges in our work and, often, in relation to others at work. And we can find ways to support each other in moving into and through these challenges, and journey through them together as appropriate and necessary.

One thing to consider in the context of convergence and chaos is the role that differences in consciousness play. Consider two converging rivers again for a moment. One of them flows from a clear lake, along a clean, clear rock-bottomed riverbed. The other comes from a murky lake along a silty bed. When they converge, the clear water will meet the murky water, and something new will happen. Will the water resolve into clarity or murkiness, or something in between? Extending this metaphor, we may come into a relationship with clarity, focus, and energy and encounter the other who brings less of all of these—a recipe for a certain kind of chaos.

Business is not only a context for cultivating awareness, but for pursuing one's purpose with passion, energy, and focus—and it requires effectiveness and productivity. So we can work with murky water to some extent, within the parameters of our principles and commitments, but also with clear, explicit limits and boundaries.

There are two principal approaches to working with chaos that I know and practice. The first is to observe it with mindfulness, as you would watch anything else; after all, all is chaos to some extent—it is just a matter of degrees of intensity. Chaos in the workplace has many forms: from initial brainstorming sessions on a new project to unexpected crises in the face of looming production deadlines. In these circumstances we can become disoriented and resistant, or we can ride the chaos like a steady boat on a rocky sea, moving up and down with the waves, witnessing the motion but staying out of the water. The more you practice mindfulness, the more skillful you will be at applying it in increasingly challenging circumstances. Through mindfulness, you can observe chaos until it passes or gives way to something else.

The other approach—the process approach—is to find the energy in the chaos and move with it, amplifying it, playing with it, dancing with it like riding the rapids down a river, until it resolves and reveals the hidden potential it was carrying. In this approach, we mindfully acknowledge the presence of chaos and we stir it up. In some companies I know, where there is deep trust and awareness, colleagues allow themselves to yell, scream, and even curse at one another in some meetings—much like the Yanomami chiefs do when their tribes converge. This is like diving off the boat and into the water, with the confidence that at some point the water will calm down—and it inevitably does.

In both cases, we begin by acknowledging that we are experiencing chaos and, rather than avoiding it or pushing it away, we open to it. Of course, if the chaos we experience is truly beyond us, poses a danger to us, or is simply unnecessary, we can remove ourselves or take steps to calm the chaos. But the chaos I refer to is the state of fluid, uncontrolled creativity that holds potential for connection, collaboration, and creation.

With respect to our relationships with other people and groups, rather than trying to control them, we can influence them and—if they accept our influence—guide them in certain directions. Influence is a way out of chaos and into co-creation. It is built upon trust and relationship.

DEEP LISTENING

> *To be with another in this way means that for the time being, you lay aside your own views and values in order to enter another's world without being prejudiced. In some sense it means that you lay aside your self; this can only be done by persons who are secure enough in themselves that they know they will not get lost in the world of the other, and that they can comfortably return to their own world when they wish.*
>
> —CARL ROGERS

Listening is the bridge between internal and external. It is the way we cultivate awareness—receiving information from inside and out—to inform our understanding. It is the starting point for connecting our awareness with that of others, for building shared understanding and, ultimately, collaborative action.

Listening from the heart is more than hearing. It is sensing through many channels and truly embracing what is calling to be heard. Listening is an invitation, an opening, a gift we give to others. If we truly listen from our hearts, then greed, aversion, and delusion do not interfere. We suspend our thoughts, fears, wants, and needs for the moment and open to those of one another. Of course, we do not abandon our own considerations, and if the other self-indulgently abuses our invitation, we have to return to our self-interest and shift out of full listening. But listening in this way opens the space for true connection.

The outcome of a conversation based in deep listening is as distinct as night and day from that of one that is not. We often don't even pretend to listen, but simply dictate through our words or actions. If we are in a position of authority or influence over others, we may receive no resistance from such dictating. Sometimes orders and responses to them are appropriate—but more often than not, inquiry into the perspective of others and truly listening to their responses will uncover hidden jewels of insight and information that those others may not even have been aware of.

Deep listening, or listening from the heart, does not come naturally to many of us, nor is it something we are typically taught. The listening most of us learn by example is more like a competitive sport or a debate. We can barely contain ourselves (and we often don't) until the other person is finished talking. We are neither interested in what others have to say nor do we allow space to really hear them, as we hold on to our own perspective—afraid to lose to theirs before we even understand it.

This pattern creates a vicious cycle of offense and defense, which inhibits both of us from understanding one another. We may not even really know where *we* stand, as we are so identified with holding on or defending that we can't explore our own needs and interests clearly and thoughtfully.

Sometimes I observe myself getting impatient and hurrying conversations. Invariably, if I slow down and listen to others, they will slow down too, and what they say will be more meaningful. They will be more connected to the conversation and more invested in its outcome, and the relationship will be enriched.

Deep listening requires genuine interest in others and in what they wish or need to express. Cultivating this interest, or developing awareness of our interest in others, is a key step. What is their experience? What are their motivations, their dreams? How do their motivations and dreams relate to mine? Slowing down, opening up, and listening to another is one of the greatest acts of compassion and greatest gifts we can give. And it is a powerful tool for connecting and building trust that leads to productive collaboration.

Exercise: Deep Listening

Here is a simple (though not necessarily easy) three-step process to facilitate deep listening. Underlying each step is the key to connection—awareness. You can do this exercise with another person or by yourself.

Let's begin with awareness. Get into a comfortable position and take a few breaths. Relax your jaw and shoulders. Elevate your spine. And breathe.

Imagine you are with someone you work with who is difficult for you. Perhaps you have different opinions, or you do things differently, or you are competitive with each other. In any case, you are called upon to make a decision together. What do you do?

Step one: Observe judgment As you engage with this person, notice any judgments that come up for you. Hear the voice in your head telling you its stories about this person and his or her ideas.

Step two: Suspend judgment Even if you are right, let it go. You don't have to let it go forever or lose whatever truth may be in your stories, but put them aside for now. Totally.

Step three: Inquiry Ask yourself questions about this person and her perspective. Where is she coming from? Why might she think the way she does? How might your behavior influence the way she thinks and acts? Ask her meaningful questions to draw out authentic answers that can help you to understand her and her perspective. Really *listen* to her responses.

Envision opportunities you have to apply this in your work, for real, in the face of a challenging person or in a challenging situation. And go for it!

WISE SPEECH

In due season will I speak.
Truthfully will I speak.
Gently, conducive of concord, not harshly will I speak.
With clear intention will I speak.
To their benefit will I speak.
These are the marks of speech, which is
well-spoken, blameless and above reproach.

—THE BUDDHA

When and how we speak, what we say or don't say, and why
we say what we do inform our communication as significantly as does the receptivity of the listener.

Words are powerful agents of meaning. We can choose
them with care and attention, or not. We can use them to
build bridges of understanding or walls of separation. Our
words reflect our thoughts, which reflect our way of viewing
the world and our judgments and preconceptions. Do we
ask people if they will share their thoughts and insights with
us, or do we "pick their brain"? Do we explore relationships
with prospective customers, or do we look to penetrate the
market segment? The tone, volume, and intention of our
voices, and the messages our body conveys as we speak, all
inform our connection in conversation.

Gossip—talking about others who are not present—is
a damaging and destructive use of speech that shows up
in business, as in all other aspects of life. It seems to be
hardwired into us. In business, especially in the context of
conflicts or controversies, gossip runs rampant and fuels the
fires of conflict and confusion. Sometimes it can take the
form of venting about what someone has said or done, or

about how we feel we are being treated, which is often a highly charged expression of emotion. While we may intend to disperse our feelings and clear the way for healthier, more productive communication, venting is often like spreading a virus. It doesn't disappear simply because we spilled it out, but transfers to others in an insidious way, affecting their perception of or relationship to the person we vent about, or to us, or both. By venting about how we were more deserving of a promotion than someone else or how the group decision was wrong or some other difference, we move away from, rather than into, connection.

Wise speech is unquestionably among the hardest of practices to master. We are so deeply conditioned to just let rip, and most of us have little training, modeling, or peer support to restrain ourselves in our speech. There are big differences between telling a lie and exercising restraint, and between the whole truth and the constructive truth. Just because we see or know something about someone does not mean we need to express it. Discernment is a sign of maturity and wisdom, especially when it involves gossip.

Exercise: Managing Gossip

This exercise for managing gossip is similar to the last exercise on deep listening. Once again, underlying each step is awareness.

Find a comfortable position and take a few breaths. Relax your jaw and shoulders. Extend your spine. And breathe.

Imagine that you have been having an issue with someone you work with and you are with coworkers.

You are about to start talking about the person and your problem with him.

Step one: Observe your thoughts and catch yourself. You don't have to stop your thoughts, but you do need to see them and realize that you are about to express them.

Step two: Process your thoughts on your own or ask the person in question if he or she will have a conversation with you. Sometimes we can work through issues we have with other people on our own, since half the problem usually resides within us. Other times it serves to engage directly with the person. If you decide to engage, then practice deep listening and, ideally, set clear intentions and guidelines for your conversation—for yourself and between the two of you.

Step three: Ask for facilitation support. If you are not successful working through the issue yourselves, or if you prefer not to try to do so, ask for facilitation or mediation to help you communicate with each other and work through your issue.

If people start to gossip to you about others who are not present, observe your inclination to join in, catch yourself, and suggest they follow the same process.

Envision opportunities you have to apply this in your work. And go for it!

Entering into Dialogue

Dialogue is a particular form of communication in which we listen deeply and respond authentically, building on awareness to collectively foster an emerging new awareness. The Greek origins of the word can be translated as "flowing through meaning." Dialogue is the process of connecting through authentic communications, using words and other channels, in which we truly hear and feel the intent of the other person's message, and we feel heard in the same way—addressing each other as "I" and "Thou" and co-creating meaning. When we communicate in this way, trust and connections deepen, relationships flourish, and collaboration ensues, releasing creativity and productive energy.

The late David Bohm, a world-renowned physicist, was also a deep humanist and passionately interested in how human beings connect and co-create meaning. In the early 1980s, in collaboration with Donald Factor and Peter Garrett, Bohm formalized the process known as Bohm Dialogue, a group process that fosters understanding of how we think and relate to one another and that facilitates group thinking. Building on Bohm's work and drawing from other sources, Peter Winchell outlines in his book *Rules of the Dialogue Game* "ten easy rules for creating more enjoyable, productive, enlightening conversations," which provide a useful framework for entering into dialogue.

> *Rule 1: It's a Time-Out.* We consciously decide to create a safe space for our conversation outside of the hustle and bustle of everyday activity.
>
> *Rule 2: No Right or Wrong Answers.* No judgments in dialogue. No winners or losers. No interrogations, only inquiries. Open exploration of thoughts is welcome.

Rule 3: Make No Decisions. Pure dialogue is not aimed at any outcome other than thinking together and building understanding. While we can use dialogue to lead to informed, collaborative decisions, in itself it is designed to be open-ended, not goal-directed.

Rule 4: You May Pass. You can ask any questions you like. And you can choose not to speak.

Rule 5: Think in New Ways. Explore. Take risks. Be flexible.

Rule 6: Ask Interesting Questions. Ask open-ended questions that elicit thoughtful answers, rather than questions that call for a "yes or no" answer. Ask authentic questions—ones you care about the answer to.

Rule 7: Maximize Cohesion. Ask questions and make comments that draw others into the conversation. Synthesize understanding to elevate the group mind. Draw out what each participant has to offer.

Rule 8: Honor Diversity. Embrace the richness of diversity and look for the synergies resulting from unique combinations.

Rule 9: Treat Each Other as Colleagues. Convene as friends in conversation, as equals among equals. Respect and challenge each other to call out the best in each other. Distinguish thoughts from people.

Rule 10: Everyone Wins! Through dialogue we all win as we express new aspects of ourselves, make new connections with each other, and co-create new meaning in a safe, enjoyable, and productive way.

Many of the principles inherent in Bohm Dialogue and the Dialogue Game can be found and applied in other forms of dialogue, and the system can be modified to facilitate particular agendas and reach desired outcomes.

Council Process: Council has a deep tradition among the indigenous peoples of North America, as well as other cultures throughout the world. In its essence, it is a form of group process and cultivates a powerful group field, calling forth the group's wisdom both through the voices of its members and through their silence. In its traditional form, a talking stick is passed around a circle and only the person holding the stick speaks—or chooses not to speak. People speak from the heart, attentive to the group field and to the words that call to be spoken. The others listen, deeply and completely, letting go of their own agenda and position.

Simple yet powerful rules—speaking from the heart, listening from the heart, respect for the group (which can mean brevity in speaking), spontaneity, and confidentiality—support group members to speak openly, honestly, respectfully, and constructively. Native American tribes use council to address the deepest, most significant decisions. In what is described as an almost magical process, in which what is being said often seemingly has nothing to do with the issue at hand, the group winds its way around and around the circle until the decision reveals itself. A consistent, ongoing practice of holding council can be a powerful way to support the development of a group and support unfolding awareness and connection.

Stringing the Beads: I learned this practice from Cheryl Fields Tyler, founder of Blue Beyond Consulting, whose team is co-creating the Accelerating Women Entrepreneurs campaign with the FLOW team. Cheryl will often dedicate an hour or more of a team meeting to this process, especially if it is early in the life of the group. The idea is to build community by deepening knowledge, understanding, and awareness about one another. The process is fairly simple and straightforward and draws on the principles of council.

We begin by taking turns, giving a brief autobiography and then addressing a question such as "What is one moment or experience from my past that played a role in leading me to this moment, with this group, connected to the purpose we are convened around?" After one round, we might address another question or reflect on the stories of the other people in the circle. Taking time to string the beads of our personal stories connects us to one another, clarifies our connection to our purpose, and helps build a collective story.

Nonviolent Communication: One of the key tools of Nonviolent Communication—a practice developed by Marshall Rosenberg—is reflective listening. Working with another person, we ask a series of questions, and after each of their responses we mirror back to them what we heard until they feel fully understood—"Yes, that is what I meant to communicate." After we complete a round of getting clear with one voice as the lead speaker, we switch roles. There is no judgment in this process, just reflection and refinement. Repeated expression and reflection refines both expression and listening, and deepens shared understanding.

Let's use Bob and Ann as an example. Since they have to work together for the new product launch to succeed, they need to find a way to get past their impasse in understanding each other. Here is a sample dialogue between them, first without employing reflective listening.

Ann: "Bob, I need your budget. Now!"

Bob: "Geez, Ann, you know we're pressed for time if we're going to hit our deadline. Can't it wait until next week?"

Ann: "The way your team is running through money, we could be in hot water by next week."

Bob: "No product, no sales. No sales, no money."

Okay, these two are clearly hot with each other. Now let's see how we can change even a heated conversation like this by employing reflective listening. Note that in some cases it serves to have a facilitator monitoring and "enforcing" this method.

Ann: "Bob, I need your budget. Now!"

Bob: "Okay, Ann. I hear that you need my budget now. Can we take a few minutes for a conversation, so we can find a time for me to get it to you that works for both of us?"

Ann: "Sure."

Bob: "What is your timing on the budget?"

Ann: "ASAP."

Bob: "Okay, I hear that you want it right away."

Ann: "That's right."

Bob: "Why is it so pressing that you have it right away?"

Ann: "Our cash flow is really tight right now and I need to know what we will be laying out in the next few weeks."

Bob: "I get it. Cash flow is tight, and you want to manage it carefully and not get into a squeeze."

Ann: "That's right."

Bob: "So, would it be helpful and sufficient for now if I got you a list of the requisitions we need to make in the next two weeks?"

Ann: "Actually, that would be great."

Exercise: Practicing Dialogue

Dialogue begins with awareness, openness, and listening. We can experience dialogue within ourselves by tuning in to our multiple internal voices, which the late renowned psychologist Fritz Perls referred to as the Voices. We might think we have a single, consistent perspective about things when in fact, on almost every issue, we have multiple voices inside vying for attention and prominence. They reflect our multiple roles and the range of our perspectives from the point of view of any role. Now let's try an experiment.

Find a comfortable position and take a few breaths. Relax your jaw and shoulders. Extend your spine. And breathe.

Consider scenarios such as these: you are starting a new business, with all the time and energy that involves; you are in a new burgeoning relationship, or you and your partner just had a baby. (Or choose a similar scenario you can relate to.) Your doctor has just told you that you have to exercise at least one hour a day for the health of your heart. So there you are: an entrepreneur, a mate, and a person concerned about your health.

Now look at the voice connected with each of these roles. Imagine what the voice connected with each has to say about how you spend your time. What does the entrepreneur have to say? How does the entrepreneur feel about the pressure from your mate or from the doctor?

What does the voice of your role as a mate or a parent say? And what about the voice of a person whose health has been jeopardized by the stress? What do they have to say to each other and to the entrepreneur or change agent in you?

Recognizing multiple points of view within ourselves helps us recognize the multiple views others hold within themselves, and those that may be going on in our conversations.

Dialogue Assignment: Invite one of the groups you work with, or convene a new group, to join you in a regular dialogue process. You can follow the rules of the Dialogue Game, hold a council, or start your meetings by "stringing the beads." But consciously employ one of these and keep track of how the group is affected by this heightened level of conscious conversation. You can also set up an ongoing reflective listening process with one or more of your colleagues to deepen listening and inquiry and cultivate understanding and trust.

Conversations with Crowds:
A Dialogue with the World

The Internet and social media add a new dimension to connecting. While telephones and other communication tools have facilitated real-time communication for decades, the new tools expand our opportunities for connecting and create opportunities for richly textured communications, even with large groups.

The ability to navigate cyberspace seems to be hardwired into the current generation. Indian physicist Sugata Mitra tested his belief that illiterate kids living in poverty can quickly and easily become computer-literate and, subsequently, literate. He embedded a computer, connected to the Internet, in a concrete wall in an alley in New Delhi, with a video camera and remote computer monitoring its use. He found that within days, young ghetto kids had taught themselves to draw on the computer and browse the Net, with no guidance or instruction. This experiment represents a groundswell of activity under way to provide computer and Internet access to billions of disenfranchised people throughout the world.

The ubiquitous search for meaning and connection is palpable in the social media sphere. The nature of Web sites and the way people use them reflect a quest for community, connection, and purpose. As Barack Obama's presidential campaign and countless cause-related campaigns demonstrate, the new media provide tremendous opportunities for catalyzing collective action.

We have the opportunity to tap into the self-organizing nature of online communities and catalyze collaborative community in our businesses and other purposeful endeavors. The immediacy and ubiquity of the technology can provide almost instantaneous feedback from the marketplace, supporting the creation of companies and the iteration of products and services that find their audience because their audience co-creates them. So much access and choice, speed of communications, and volume of information—as well as the virtual nature of relationships in cyberspace—means that we are challenged to sustain focus and interest and cultivate depth within our communities.

While many of the new social-media technology tools inherently foster communication and connection, communications and actions that emerge from them can be superficial and even dangerous without a conscious culture of connection. By employing awareness practice and conscious culture, we have the opportunity to leverage new media to foster conscious community in our businesses and social enterprises. Companies large and small are creating internal wikis and other collaborative platforms to facilitate conscious communication and collaboration. After instituting "Facebook Fridays," in which team members communicate with each other through their personal Facebook pages, Serena Software CEO Jeremy Burton noticed an immediate and ongoing transformation of the company's culture—from one with little communication to a culture of collaboration. If we engage in authentic dialogue with these communities and are open to what they may co-create with us, we have the opportunity to catalyze extraordinary creativity and energy.

While reading books is on the decline (the attention span of young readers tends to be measured in moments and paragraphs, rather than hours and pages) and streaming video seems to be preferable to scrolling text for the younger generations, words still matter, whether written or spoken.

A few kind words, acknowledgments, and appreciations, even in an email, are warmly received and enthusiastically embraced. As the pace of communications accelerates and the volume of information expands, communicating considerately, reaching out with questions, and reflecting genuine interest foster connection that goes way beyond the realm of the communication platform we happen to use.

SUMMARY: CONNECTION

> *Between stimulus and response, there is a space. In that space lies our freedom and power to choose our response. In our response lies our growth and freedom.*
>
> —VIKTOR FRANKL

Awareness coupled with interest and compassion is the source of connection. We co-create reality with others as we co-create each other.

We create the context for infinite possibilities when we observe the sensations, feelings, thoughts, and intuition that might create walls between ourselves and others, hold these in suspense, and open to the other person without judgment.

We build trust and confidence by authentically and transparently embodying our passion, intentions, purpose, and principles and by fulfilling our commitments. We build a dependable practice of connecting by explicitly putting our agendas aside to be present with each other and by employing simple yet effective tools that facilitate listening and dialogue.

Even when we are feeling stressed or threatened, we have the opportunity to exercise awareness and sustain connection. I just had an experience that illustrates this point. I've been working on a project with a colleague for the past few weeks, and today is the day we are to deliver it. Discussing it on the phone with my colleague, I reached saturation point: I had no more time I was willing to invest in the project, as it was compromising my ability to do the many other things that called for my attention. After I expressed this several times and my colleague kept adding issues to consider, I felt myself heating up inside, and I expressed what was going on for me—even as I acknowledged that I heard what she was saying. I said I did not mean to be disrespectful or inappropriate, but I had to stop because I was reaching the point of undermining my ability to deliver on commitments I had made to myself and others—a bottom line for me.

I allowed myself to express my intense feelings, confirmed my commitment to her, our process, our relationship, and staying connected (which she acknowledged) while facilitating the completion of our project with an agreement about where we are and where we will go next. Maintaining awareness and connection in the heat of passion and stress is essential to sustaining healthy, productive collaboration. And while I could have taken a break, meditated, and otherwise chilled out (which is not a bad idea!), I chose to sustain awareness and connection even when my temperature rose.

Writing Reflection: Connection

Take a moment to tune in. Take a few deep breaths and observe how you are seated. Feel yourself, and reflect on these questions.

How do you best connect?

_____

_____

_____

What are the connecting skills you are best at?

_____

_____

Which ones would you like to develop more fully?

_____

_____

How do you like to be connected to?

_____

_____

To what extent can you let others know this and help them learn how to do so with you?

_____

_____

What connecting practices do you want to bring into your work team? How can you envision doing so?

_____

_____

_____

_____

Chapter Five

COLLABORATION

No one can whistle a symphony. It takes
a whole orchestra to play it.

—H. E. LUCCOCK

C arl is a senior leader at a well-respected, global bio-
tech company, faced with the task of integrating the
company's network of site-based human resources
departments into a global system with shared resources—
without losing quality of service or delivery capability. The
company's history of processing major changes of this nature
and scale has been very poor, resulting in lower morale and
widespread negative attitudes. Not surprisingly, Carl encounters strong resistance when he talks to colleagues within the
company about the process he is charged with managing.

In the past, Carl would not have considered the company's history as he approached his task. He would have
designed and implemented a change plan based on the outcome he envisioned, without paying attention to the effect

of the unconscious in change processes. But he has been receiving collaboration training over the past year, and what he has learned leads him to design a process of discovery and collaboration, rather than one of command and control.

He starts with an extensive series of one-on-one meetings with all of the stakeholders he has identified as having the ability to block the change process. He institutes collaboration training for the disparate human resources teams, and periodic meetings of individual site-based teams. He has also set group meetings with all the team leaders, facilitated by an outside collaboration consultant. Through this process Carl experiences himself as a co-creator with the team leaders and team members. He has a clear sense of who his allies are and who will require special attention and enrollment. The result of this collaborative process is a successful integration process resulting in a higher level of service and enhanced team morale.

Collaboration: The act of working together to create or produce something; reflecting common aspirations by sharing responsibility and learning together.

Collaboration is where the rubber meets the road—where Working for Good becomes working together. Where connection means meeting each other as whole beings, turning connection into action: taking its electricity and turning on the lights with it. Collaboration requires all the skills and practices we have cultivated so far in this book.

One of my collaborators, Elad Levinson, views collaboration as an ongoing conversation punctuated by a series of smaller conversations. To continue the water metaphor, we can view it as many streams merging into one big one. At times we even plunge over waterfalls together, creating a new level of chaos with dramatic expressions of creativity and releases of energy. And just as it does with connection, the chaos leads to a new flow: a bigger, better oxygenated river.

In this chapter, for continuity, we will explore collaboration through the story of Sue, the social entrepreneur who is catalyzing a new program designed to deliver empowerment education to inner-city youth. She has extensive experience in youth empowerment education and sees a great need for a new kind of program that integrates health, fitness, leadership training, and service work, while attracting broad attention and widespread support for the program and the young people going through it.

By following her unfolding story, we will explore how to apply awareness practices to collaboration, and how embodied awareness—directional, focused intention guided by principles—comes together with the skills of connection to foster collaboration. Sue's process, and the skills she employs, can apply to any entrepreneur, change agent, or person committed to Working for Good. Jack the tech entrepreneur relies on collaboration to ensure that his high-performance teams are in sync. Jocelyn the artist relies on collaboration to produce her community events. And collaboration is the foundation of Evan the project manager's work.

Exercise: Tuning In to Collaboration
Find a comfortable position. Take a few deep breaths. Feel your jaw and your shoulders drop as you exhale.

With each inhale, feel your spine lengthen. Quickly scan your body to sense if there is any tension. If you find some, breathe into it and observe it. Then move on.

Recall or imagine a collaboration setting that is easy and flowing. It can be as simple or complex as you choose. Observe the situation. What does it look like? Feel like? What role are you playing? Who else is participating? What are the factors that make it easy?

Let this story go and take a few full breaths.

Now recall or imagine a collaboration setting that is challenging. Again, it can be as simple or complex as you choose. Observe the situation. What does it look like? Feel like? What role are you playing? Who else is participating? What are the factors that make it difficult? How are you showing up? How are others responding to you? What can you do to make the situation easier?

Let this story go, take a few full breaths, and take a little time to compare the stories. What was different between the easy and difficult one? What made one easy and the other difficult?

Take a couple of breaths, and let the experience go.

SUE GETS STARTED: RECOGNITION AND INTERNAL EXPLORATION

Never doubt that a small group of thoughtful, committed citizens can change the world. Indeed, it is the only thing that ever has.

—MARGARET MEAD

Like any entrepreneur, Sue is on fire. She is inspired by a vision of helping thousands of young people find their passion and purpose, develop appropriate skills, and access appropriate resources to pursue their dreams. And she sees an opportunity to accomplish this in a new way, through a new program she has created—at least in her mind.

Sue knows that a first step toward manifesting her vision is to clearly frame and articulate it so she can present it to others, receive their feedback, and engage their support. She also knows that articulating her vision—writing and talking about it—clarifies, refines, and makes it more tangible. And she knows she needs to attract support from people whose talents complement hers and who cover areas that are beyond her expertise. She writes:

Intentions: My intention is to apply my experience, talent, time, energy, relationships, and other resources to build an organization that supports young people in difficult settings—including inner-city and other areas where there is little social and economic opportunity. I intend to develop a unique program that addresses all aspects of the participants, including their physical, intellectual, emotional, and spiritual health and well-being. To ensure success for the participants and sustainability for the program, I will develop in collaboration with others a complete ecosystem of support, including financial institutions that can provide seed capital for participants' entrepreneurial projects, mentors to provide ongoing support and counsel, companies that can provide jobs to other program graduates, and government agencies and NGOs to provide funding and other resources. Success breeds success, and by telling the success stories of program participants and graduates, we will attract greater numbers of participants and ongoing support from many organizations across sectors. In keeping with the aim of the program—to foster healthy, well-balanced, productive, and happy people—even as my team and I work intensely and diligently to realize these intentions, we will maintain balance and health in our own lives and realize meaningful benefits—material, emotional, psychological, and otherwise—for ourselves.

YEP! – Youth Empowerment Project

Purpose: To create a conscious community and culture of opportunity that supports young people in developing the skills, mind-set, and network of support to find their passion and purpose, and to pursue their dreams with confidence, skill, and success.

Principles: Given that the underlying intentions and purpose of YEP! include catalyzing personal empowerment, conscious community, and overall health and well-being for all involved, we will embody the following principles in our work: authenticity, transparency, open-heartedness, reciprocity and mutual support, compassion, collaboration, and servant leadership.

Once she gets her core ideas down clearly, Sue begins to identify people she knows whose work, experience, and interests align with the purpose of YEP! and with whom she feels aligned; she starts having conversations with them about the program. She also identifies themes, issues, and opportunities relevant to developing the program and looks to identify other people who can address these.

When Collaboration Works

If we think about it, we collaborate all of the time. Likewise, most of us live in relative peace most of the time; that is, we aren't fighting or at war. Peace, like collaboration, is relative, and we experience it to varying degrees and at different levels. In working with sensitive people, I've found that if I raise my voice a few decibels or use it forcefully, even if quietly, I might get "Is there something wrong? Are you upset about something?" They can feel and reflect the force of my expression regardless of its intensity. And intensity does not have to be violent; in the story I recounted earlier of the intense phone conversation in which I explicitly expressed and "owned" my intense feelings, I made it clear that I was expressing my inner stress and, while I did ask my colleague to shift with me, I did not abuse or belittle her in the process.

Families, communities, and the global marketplace all require constant collaboration and cooperation, most of which is unconscious—built into the fabric of coexistence. We collaborate one-on-one, one-with-many, and one-among-many. The underlying cultural norms, the basic trust, understanding, and relationships we have with others, and the mutual benefit facilitated by the inherent nature of social groups and the voluntary exchange in the marketplace foster a culture of collaboration.

Collaboration has many faces and tones. We collaborate out of necessity for survival and mechanically in compliance with social norms. We collaborate to ingratiate ourselves with others, feel good about ourselves, establish our social position, and fulfill our drive to serve. And we collaborate because we are called to do so—to share in becoming more human and realizing more of our individual and collective potential. If we want to change the world and serve as agents of change within business, we must collaborate consciously and effectively.

Collaboration becomes an issue when it is challenging and when it needs to be conscious and explicit: to address complex issues, overcome conflicts, and make difficult decisions together. Collaboration to explore new territory, create together, and bring new vision to life frequently evokes creative tension, confrontation, and challenges. And collaboration requires a degree of intimacy, which stirs things up and takes us to our edges as our psyche, ego, and perspectives are confronted by those of others.

In the context of Working for Good, with our commitment to manifesting more conscious behavior in business and fostering individual and collective growth and development, collaboration is essential. It is the platform for putting our skills of awareness and connection into practice. Without the need to collaborate, we can simply dream of our visions of a better world and grandiose accomplishments. But as soon as we begin working to manifest our visions and pursue action, we encounter other people with *their* visions and pursuits, as well as egos, personalities, and behavior patterns. While some people are easier for us to work with than others, all require some degree of attention, energy, and accommodation on our part.

We seek to understand the ingredients of successful collaboration and facilitation so we can apply them to foster successful collaboration in challenging contexts, maintain and reestablish flow when it is blocked, and increase our ability to be present and effective.

SUE STEPS OUT: EXTENDING THE INVITATION

> *The leaders who work most effectively, it seems to me, never say "I." And that's not because they have trained themselves not to say "I." They don't think "I." They think "we"; they think "team." They understand their job to be to make the team function. They accept responsibility and don't sidestep it, but "we" gets the credit. This is what creates trust, what enables you to get the task done.*
>
> —PETER DRUCKER

Based on her initial on-on-one conversations, Sue has identified a few highly aligned and interested colleagues, and is now ready to convene a meeting. She invites three people to convene for a ninety-minute meeting, with three objectives or desired outcomes: to develop a shared understanding of the purpose of YEP! and how it will fulfill its purpose, to build the relationships between the four participants, and to agree on specific next steps for advancing the project and what role each participant will play in them.

Sue introduces the participants to one another via email and proposes some times and locations for the meeting. After a few exchanges, all agree on a time and place. Next, she proposes an agenda, which includes:

- *"Tuning in":* asking if anyone would like to prepare a ritual or statement to open the meeting
- *Ground rules:* listening from the heart, speaking from the heart, brevity, and confidentiality. No pressure to participate beyond the meeting
- *"Stringing the beads":* which she briefly describes

- *Discussion of the concept of YEP!:* its purpose and her vision of how it can work and why it is timely
- *Exploration of next steps:* identifying others to include in the conversation and development process
- *Agreement on next steps, roles, and responsibilities*
- *Meeting review*
- *Appreciations*

The others all agree to the agenda.

In her work thus far, Sue has already begun to employ and model facilitation skills, including engaging all of the participants, fostering small agreements, and establishing a clear framework for both the meeting and the ongoing collaboration.

The Art of Facilitation: Harnessing the Wisdom of the Group

Facilitate means "to make easy." Facilitation is the art and practice of making collaboration easy (or easier), and facilitative behaviors foster ease of movement through even the most challenging passages. Facilitation presupposes our intention to collaborate, our interest in doing so without getting mired in conflict, and our commitment to authentic relationship and individual and collective growth. Facilitation catalyzes the wisdom of the group and fosters decisions that engage the hearts and minds of all involved in order to generate unified action.

The objective of facilitation and collaboration is to establish shared responsibility for success. To be successful, our meetings and other collaboration platforms need to lead to informed decisions and clear action steps that advance the aims of our larger collaboration. The process needs to engage participants and facilitate information exchange and decision-making, and relationships need to be characterized by mutual respect and honesty—and be strengthened through the process.

Facilitative behaviors foster the flow of collaboration. Some set the context for ease of collaboration. The practices of self-awareness, deep listening, dialogue, and wise speech are fundamentally facilitative behaviors. Making and keeping to our agreements are also facilitative behaviors. Establishing clearly defined roles and decision-making processes are highly facilitative, as they establish a clear context for collaboration. Checking in with one another to ensure that we are on the same page, suspending our judgments, and asking one another to do the same are facilitative.

Other facilitative behaviors serve to restore ease when it is disrupted. Interventions include reinforcing the ground rules and agreements we set to guide our collaboration, engaging the group in addressing challenging questions, and checking in to see whether members are in the same place or if the group needs to realign itself in some way. Slowing down is almost always facilitative, unless the group process clearly calls for speeding up.

We can embody facilitative behaviors whether we are serving as a facilitator or participating in a collaboration and addressing the challenges and conflicts in it.

Principle: Integrity

Things with integrity tend to hold together, persist, and have a coherent identity as a whole. A tree has integrity, with its root and its branches seamlessly connected to its trunk.

Larry Pentoney was one of the wisest and most experienced of my business mentors over the years. He was a senior vice president at Sterling Pharmaceuticals and, among other things, built and managed its businesses in Brazil and Spain. One of the key lessons Larry taught me was to always bundle responsibility, authority, and accountability together.

For people to effectively embody their position and succeed in the tasks they are charged with, they must be empowered with all three elements—responsibility, authority, and accountability—in appropriate measure. Responsibility or accountability without authority is a recipe for frustration and discontent. Authority without responsibility or accountability is a formula for abuse. The three combined manifest integrity.

Integrity is an essential element for effective facilitation and leadership. It inspires self-confidence in the facilitator/leader as well as participants' confidence in him or her. In addition to the integrity derived from the appropriate measure of responsibility, authority, and accountability, facilitators and leaders need to embody the integrity that comes from congruency between their principles, commitments, and actions.

<hr />

SUE CONVENES THE FIRST MEETING: INITIATING COLLABORATION

If your actions inspire others to dream more, learn more, do more and become more, you are a leader.

—JOHN QUINCY ADAMS

Sue begins the meeting by asking if anyone has any questions or comments before the group formally begins, and she makes a comment about her role as an "invested" facilitator: she will be facilitating the meeting with an intention to be neutral, but she acknowledges that she has a vested interest in the outcome of the meeting as well as opinions and insights she will want to contribute, which a purely neutral facilitator might not have. She adds that others may step into the role of facilitator as appropriate. Finally, she remarks that the agenda is flexible, not fixed: it is meant to support a process to meet the desired outcomes, but it is subject to change as they proceed—with the consent of the participants. "Is this clear?" she asks, and when the others acknowledge she proceeds.

One of the participants picks up on Sue's earlier invitation and offers to lead a moment of silence with a guided visualization, which tunes the participants in to their hearts and one another. When he is finished, Sue briefly reviews the agenda and ground rules, and asks if anyone has anything he or she would like to add. One of the participants asks for a clarification. Sue responds, and after he acknowledges that he understands, she asks again: "Anything else?" When they indicate no, she asks, "So we're all on the same page?" They all indicate that they are.

Sue then invites them to begin "stringing the beads" by taking turns to briefly introduce themselves in a way that is relevant to the purpose of YEP! and to tell a story that reflects their passion for empowering disadvantaged youth. John, an educator, tells his story about teaching in a remote village in Africa in the Peace Corps and seeing "the lights go on" for impoverished young people; Ellen, a psychotherapist, tells her story about working with kids traumatized by abuse and family violence, and seeing hope and faith rekindled. Allen tells his story about managing social programs in New York City and humanizing a bureaucracy in the process; and Sue tells her story about how the vision for the YEP! program came to her and how it makes sense based on her history, passion, and intentions.

Sue suggests that, as a next round, each person comment on what came up for them as they heard the others' stories, and all agree. After that, they talk freely for a brief while. Then Sue acknowledges what an amazing group of people they are, and how appropriate they all are as "midwives" for YEP!, and she asks if they are ready to move on to the next item on the agenda. They agree, and Sue initiates a discussion of the concept of YEP!

Sue explains her multidisciplinary approach based on teams of instructors working with teams of young people, who will learn individual and group skills including self-care, meditation, deep listening and dialogue, collaboration, and facilitation. She goes on to explain her approach to the "business" of the program, leveraging foundation and school district funds and engaging corporate partners who are active in the community and sell products to young people, and who can provide jobs or other opportunities to qualified young people.

After a conversation about visions, with some elements being fleshed out, Allen suggests that they should look at next steps. They all agree, and Sue asks if anyone has a preference as to how to do so. Ellen asks if Sue has any ideas about the next steps. Sue thanks her and suggests that a good next step would be to convene a meeting with a larger group soon and to take some time now to plan it. She adds that, ideally, participants would come out of that next meeting with some working teams that take responsibility for developing certain aspects of the project in a coordinated way. They all enthusiastically agree and set themselves to the task.

They agree to an agenda for the next meeting and the people each will invite. Allen offers to take the lead in finding a venue for the meeting, which they anticipate will include ten to fifteen people. Sue says she will send notes from the meeting and the draft agenda for the next meeting by email the next day, and asks if anyone has anything else to add.

When they all say no, she shifts to the meeting review. "What did you like about this meeting," she asks. Comments ensue: "The people," "Your facilitation," "The project concept."

"Great. Thank you. Any more?" she asks. "OK, what would you do to make the next meeting better?" Silence. "OK, how about the duration? Was there enough time or did it take too long?" "No, it was perfect." "OK, how about the number of people?" "That worked too for this meeting." "OK, sounds like there's nothing we really need to change for now."

To close, Sue recounts a process she heard about that all of the teams at Whole Foods Market—from the produce team in a local store to the board of directors—use at the end of every meeting called Appreciations. Anyone who would like to express their appreciation to or about another person can do so in turn. "Wow," says John, "this is great. I am so thankful that you invited me and brought us all together, Sue. I think this is a great project and I am happy to be part of it." "Ditto," the others respond. "And I really appreciate how well organized this meeting was and how smoothly it flowed. Thanks to all for being so thoughtful," Allen adds. When they are all finished, Sue asks if anyone has anything to add, thanks them, and closes the meeting.

In this meeting, as she did leading up to it, Sue employed and modeled various facilitation skills, including fostering small agreements, establishing a clear and consistent process, engaging the participants, building relationships, and sticking to agreements. The meeting began and ended on time, followed the agenda, and gave everyone a voice. The process was clear and effective, and the participants built relationships and achieved desired outcomes.

Catalyzing Action

Successful meetings stimulate creativity, cultivate shared understanding, and generate good feelings, but ultimately they need to lead to action. An essential step in any meeting or collaborative process is that of clearly defining next steps—and identifying responsibility, accountability, and authority for taking those steps. Other strategies for producing coordinated action after a meeting include circulating minutes and giving people an opportunity to comment on and refine them; creating support systems for people taking action on behalf of the group, including establishing teams instead of leaving the work to an individual; evaluating the meeting itself to root out inefficiencies for the next time; and taking the time to appreciate one another's contributions before the meeting adjourns. The latter has the effect of deepening the connection between the participants and energizing them as they head back into the larger work environment.

SUE PUTS A FLAG IN THE GROUND: DEEPENING COLLABORATION AND CATALYZING A TEAM

Good leaders must first become good servants.

—ROBERT GREENLEAF

In advance of the next meeting, Sue takes a three-day workshop called "Essential Facilitation," produced by Interaction Associates, a leading consultancy on collaboration and facilitative leadership.

Building on the success of the first meeting, the new collaborative team that is coming together convenes the larger meeting, with fourteen participants representing a broad spectrum of skills and relationships relevant to YEP!

While the second meeting's agenda is more complex than the first and the stakes somewhat higher, by employing the same basic approach—in terms of structure and process, focus on balancing relationships, and results—the meeting is similarly a success. It begins with an opening ritual to connect the participants with their awareness and hearts and to their shared intention to serve and empower young people. After the opening, Sue outlines the ground rules, roles, and agenda, checking in with the participants as she goes along to ensure that any questions are addressed, that everyone understands the same thing, and that all are okay moving on. She and her initial team have designed the meeting to advance the purpose of YEP! and to effectively address the desired outcomes they have identified as essential for moving forward with the project. The agenda includes:

- *Opening ritual*
- *Start-up:* purpose, desired outcomes, agenda, ground rules
- *Introductions:* getting to know each other
- *What is empowerment?:* a conversation to elicit all participants' perspectives and come to a shared definition
- *Break*
- *YEP!:* its vision, purpose, and role
- *Lunch break*
- *Potential partners*
- *Defining action agenda:* identifying working team themes and breaking into small groups to establish specific action steps for each team
- *Small groups report back to whole group, address questions, and make refinements*
- *Establish steering committee with a representative from each working team*
- *Set next meetings*
- *Meeting review*
- *Appreciations*

Drawing on her awareness practice, the "Essential Facilitation" workshop, and her experience with Process Work, Sue employs a range of techniques to facilitate the meeting and support the group in reaching decisions together. This involves "Opening—Narrowing—Closing," a core process in the Interaction Associates system. The Opening includes brainstorming with clarification. The Narrowing includes combining closely aligned ideas that came up in the brainstorming, prioritizing, and giving people an opportunity to make the case for the ideas they feel strongly about. Closing comprises building up and eliminating options, integrating similar and compatible ideas, and ultimately acknowledging agreement.

A technique Sue uses is "weather reports": checking in with herself to see how she is feeling, reflecting it back to the group, and asking the group how they are feeling. These go something like this: "I'm feeling a little low in energy and am sensing a drop in the group's energy. I wonder if we need a break or if there is something up for anyone that we need to address."

When the group reaches moments of uncertainty—what Elad Levinson has come to call "Oh-shit" moments—Sue facilitates a process of assessing where the group is and where they want to go, and identifying steps to keep moving. True to her opening statement that the agenda is a map, not the terrain, during the meeting the group decides to shift the agenda to reflect where the group is in the moment versus a preconceived idea.

Before the meeting concludes, the groups establishes clear next steps with clearly defined responsibility, authority, and accountability.

When Collaboration Breaks Down

Skillful facilitation with a willing group is a formula for success. But not all prospective collaborations benefit from unshakeable alignment and masterful facilitation.

One danger of facilitation is the opportunity—and sometimes the inclination—to eliminate dissent and ostracize or even exclude dissenters. Another related risk of facilitation is fostering a group trance in which all "drink the Kool-Aid" and pursue an unconscious path together. And sometimes there is a fine line between facilitation and manipulation; facilitation can be used to influence a group's direction rather than activate its wisdom to co-create, or deeply inform its direction. Similarly, a masterful facilitator will always defer to awareness and the higher purpose of the collaborative process, whereas a technical facilitator who lacks deeper awareness will miss strategic opportunities for increasing the group's consciousness and cohesiveness in favor of sticking to the agenda or systematically employing a facilitation tool—without higher awareness or compassion.

Under stress, which often happens when we collaborate, a facilitator's or participant's strengths can become liabilities. For instance, if conscientiousness—the ability to responsibly get things done with purpose and direction—is among a facilitator's strengths, she may become controlling under stress, or others may perceive her that way, as she sustains her focused commitment to results. Under intense stress, being controlling can even turn into belligerence.

The presence of people operating from different levels of self-awareness can present a challenge to facilitation, and to collaboration in general. Once again we walk a fine line here, as we can view dissent as an important voice that holds wisdom to inform our overall understandings and decisions, or as self-serving disruption: and both can be true. Robb Smith, CEO of the Integral Institute, astutely observes that the nature of a collaboration is influenced by the relative levels of consciousness of the participants. If individuals or factions within the group function at different levels of embodied consciousness, prospects for easy collaboration are diminished and the likelihood of persistent conflict is high. In some situations, the facilitator may be called to require others to elevate or evacuate.

Without clearly defined roles and relationships between participants, uncertainty and insecurity trigger a veritable circus of competing individual interests and stories.

Even when a meeting or series of meetings is apparently successful, if appropriate follow-through does not ensue to advance the purpose of the collaboration, then the overall process will not be successful.

Awareness is the ultimate facilitation skill, enabling us to skillfully apply other facilitation skills. To respond effectively to challenges to collaboration, we have to see ourselves, understand our relationship to others, recognize the context and behavior patterns of others, and read both individual and unfolding group processes. Awareness is essential to recognizing the risks of facilitation, bringing them to light, and effectively addressing them.

SUE OVERCOMES ADVERSITY: SURVIVING THE RAPIDS

For the first time in the history of this campaign we are surrounded on the East, West, North, and South. We can now attack the enemy in all directions.

—GENERAL CREIGHTON WILLIAM ABRAMS,
Battle of the Bulge, WWII

During the next several months, the working teams continue to meet regularly and advance their action agendas, the steering committee has conference calls twice a month, and the whole group meets once, three months after their initial meeting. Over the course of the next six months, several new people join, and the size of the group and complexity of its process grows.

Over time, challenges and conflicts arise, which Sue has to face as facilitator. Among the issues: one of the working teams is not pulling its weight; personal agendas start to emerge and, although benefiting all involved is a core principle of the collaboration, the group is now out of balance; and individuals and working teams make decisions and communicate them to people outside the collaboration—without having the authority to make such decisions.

Sue employs a range of skills, techniques, and strategies to address these challenges. The most essential and persistent of her resources is her personal awareness practice, through which she maintains perspective and presence even in the face of adversity and stress, and which fosters keen insight and skillful responses. She also addresses challenging moments and passages by reinforcing ground rules and agreements: "Let's remember our commitment to listening from our heart and to suspending judgment and even our own thoughts to fully hear each other," and "Let's review our desired outcomes from this meeting and see if we are on track."

During one challenging time, when two people cannot come together, Sue draws on the book *Getting to Yes! Win-Win Negotiations from the Harvard Negotiation Project*. She reminds the group that to come to an agreement that serves all, they need to identify their real needs and interests (as opposed to holding on to their positions), focus on the issues instead of making people the problem, come up with options that allow everyone to win, and use objective criteria whenever possible and appropriate.

To deal with a particularly challenging person who continually asks questions that pull meetings off track, Sue uses a series of approaches including "parking lot": "Thank you for the suggestion. Since it is tangential to what we are focusing on right now, let's put it in a parking lot to address it later. We'll note it on this whiteboard and come back to it." She also uses "the boomerang" and specifically directs it to the entire group rather than the challenging participant, in order to engage the group in supporting the need to stay on track: "So, everyone, would you like to address this question now or would you prefer to do so later?" Sue even employs a technique of taking the other person's side to explore what insights might want to reveal themselves through this person (and to take the energy out of his interruptions). "If you are all okay with this, I propose we take a few minutes and really hear what Joe has to say. To make sure we're really hearing it, I will be taking his side. That is, after he says something, I will repeat it, adding expression and energy and other words to really amplify what he wants to express—checking with him as I do, to make sure I am on track."

Finally, Sue switches roles to establish a bottom line in relation to the behaviors: "I am now stepping out of my role as facilitator and expressing myself as the leader of the program, with ultimate responsibility, authority, and accountability. This line of questions and the effect it is having on the overall group dynamics and productivity are not appropriate, and I am deciding that we are done with it for now."

SUMMARY: COLLABORATION

Our ability to reach unity in diversity will be the beauty and test of our civilization.

—MAHATMA GANDHI

The promise and possibility of collaboration is joyful, playful co-creation. When the hearts, minds, and spirits of a group come together to address shared opportunities and challenges, the palette of options, ideas, and energies we employ expands, and new colors emerge from the synergies between participants.

Collaboration, like connection, often invites chaos and requires creative tension. But when facilitated with mindfulness and clear process, it leads to magnificent creativity and powerful productivity.

As facilitators and participants in collaborative process, we can employ the skills of awareness, embodiment, and connection, and the tools of facilitation to meet others in the realm of active co-creation, advancing our individual and collective interests and aspirations.

Writing Reflection: Collaboration

Give yourself a moment to tune in to your breath and your body, and to any thoughts or feelings that may come up for you, then reflect on these questions.

How do you think the idea that "awareness rules" applies to collaboration?

_____

_____

_____

_____

What facilitation skills presented in this chapter captured your attention or excited you?

_____

_____

_____

_____

How can you envision elevating the practice of collaboration in your work?

_____

_____

_____

_____

_____

What are three practical things you can apply from
this chapter to your work and how can you envision
doing so?

_____

_____

_____

_____

_____

_____

_____

_____

_____

Chapter Six

INTEGRATION

I do what I say, I say what I think, I think what I feel.
—MAHATMA GANDHI

During the entire time I wrote this book I was deeply engaged in the unfolding process of the Conscious Capitalism steering committee, which was producing our first large-scale event—a conference called "Catalyzing Conscious Capitalism." Since this was the first time we had worked together on such a project, we were simultaneously establishing the framework for an ongoing Conscious Capitalism movement and Conscious Business campaign. In spite of the substantial awareness, experience, and skills of this evolving constellation of highly intelligent, accomplished professionals, the group was fraught with tension, stress, and confrontation for many months. The interplay of egos and contrasts in personality types and leadership approaches led to a seemingly ceaseless cycle of conflict and chaos.

Growth often confronts edges or blocks, and friction comes with the territory. This was certainly a situation where growth was required from all participants, and from the committee as a whole. Personally, I was afforded the timely opportunity to put the skills of Working for Good to use.

We cultivated waves of resolution through a series of meetings and conversations including a team-building retreat. Over the course of several months, clarity slowly replaced chaos, and trust replaced conflict. In the process, roles, responsibilities, and authority were clearly defined, as were the underlying principles guiding the ongoing development of the Conscious Capitalism and Conscious Business initiatives. The success of the process was derived as much as anything from the shared intention to advance the understanding and practice of Conscious Capitalism, the opportunity for all involved to truly benefit through collaboration, and the willingness of all involved to stay with the process, in spite of the stress and discomfort along the way. The experience of working through the challenges; of explicitly addressing fears, concerns, and interests; and of working together to overcome adversity will undoubtedly provide a foundation for conscious evolution of the process over time—and will add to the experience of all involved.

This was a process that required extensive application of all of the skills of Working for Good, including rapid and ongoing integration of experiences and lessons learned, to continue the upward spiral of learning and enhancing skillfulness.

Integration: A process of combining experiences, lessons, and other elements into an integral, harmonious whole.

Integration completes the virtuous cycle of Working for Good, turning parts into a whole and giving birth to new life. Integration is essential for learning and growth; it fosters the ongoing process of unfolding awareness, which leads to new levels of embodiment, connection, and collaboration—and the spiral continues.

Integration is both an internal experience and a connecting of the internal with the external. To complete our water metaphor, integration is where the great river merges with the vast ocean, blending while maintaining its essential nature as water—individual within community, one among many, parts among the whole.

Integration involves "digesting" our experiences and incorporating the elements—lessons, ideas, insights, skills, etc.—into our being. It also requires us to recognize gaps and hindrances to our growth and development and gives us the opportunity to address them. Integration requires effort—to practice what we learn and employ it in our work—and delivers immeasurable returns.

As I mentioned earlier, since my first day on the job at FLOW three years ago, my title and role have been chief activation officer. By all external accounts, the title is appropriate, and for my part, I easily relate to it. But as I near the completion of this book, I realize how much I am drawn to embody the role of chief integration officer, as my attention and energy are increasingly focused on integration. Integration is fulfilling and energizing, like plugging in the lights after setting up the holiday decorations: you get to take in the whole experience. I suggest that we all look for opportunities to play this role in our lives and our work.

To explore integration, we begin this chapter with a review of the key concepts we have learned so far, then move into other ideas, including experiencing interdependence, measuring success, and putting the practices to work.

Review of the Key Concepts in this Book

The underlying assumptions of this book and the idea of Working for Good include the beliefs that what we do matters and who we are is relative. We are individual reflections of a greater whole, and the whole reflects who we are. We co-create one another and our shared reality. We exist as unique individuals within interdependent systems, and our businesses similarly operate within integrated systems of interdependent stakeholders. We acknowledge that life is a great unfolding mystery, and much more remains unknown than known.

Within this context, we have the opportunity to discover and cultivate an essential purpose for ourselves and our businesses, and to continually develop our consciousness and express more of our potential through our work. Key skills and actions for doing this include: cultivating our minds through awareness practice; finding and following our passion and purpose—knowing and being who we are; connecting with others by letting go of our attachments, listening deeply, and expressing ourselves authentically; caring for ourselves and others; and cultivating the skills to facilitate true dialogue and collaboration.

In this chapter we will add the elements of dealing with challenging issues and measuring success: to learn, refine, and grow.

ADDRESSING THE MISSING PIECES: BLOCKS, HOLES, AND SHADOWS

> *The ultimate measure of a man is not where he stands in moments of comfort and convenience, but where he stands at times of challenge and controversy.*
>
> —MARTIN LUTHER KING JR.

Integration calls for courageous self-reflection and cultivation. In return, it releases great energy and joy. Perhaps the greatest test of our ideas and ideals, purpose and principles, awareness and embodiment is in the way we respond to deep challenges—and among the most significant challenges we face are the aspects of ourselves we do not want to see. But what we resist persists, and to continue the cycle of increasing awareness, embodiment, connection, collaboration, and integration, we must apply the light of awareness to illuminate our deep-seated patterns of fear, grasping, and delusion.

For example, while he is normally thoughtful and inspiring, one of Rational Jack's holes is his tendency to be cold and controlling when under stress. Committed to truth and accomplishment as he is, he can lose touch with people and connection if he feels threatened. Artisan Jocelyn's passion can turn into melancholy and remorse when times get tough and she doesn't see how to shift them into a more positive pattern. In extreme circumstances, Sue the Idealist can become delusional and disconnected from reality—holding on to an idealistic fantasy rather than facing the facts. And Evan the Guardian can become almost tyrannical and brutal if he feels that order is threatened.

By reflecting on ourselves and engaging in authentic dialogue with others, we can recognize our unproductive, unconscious patterns and, with open-hearted compassion, recognize that they do not have to rule, limit, or define us. We can soften into them and understand how they serve us, both in a practical way and as teachers to guide us to new levels of self-awareness and mastery.

Jack can see how fear triggers controlling behavior and then face his fear. Jocelyn can recognize her despair as disappointed passion and reconnect with her original passion. Sue can see her disconnected delusion and readjust her vision to reflect new circumstances. And Evan can collaborate with others to establish a new construct, rather than fanatically holding on to a disintegrating old one.

Blocks, holes, and shadows show up at the level of the individual, in relationships, and in the overall functioning of a business ecosystem. We are often unaware of behaviors that contradict our intentions, principles, and commitments. Sometimes when we act unconsciously or incongruently, we are applying personal behavior patterns which may be recurrent and persistent. At other times, we may be acting out a role or imbalance in the overall system.

Among the signs indicating unaddressed missing pieces are low-quality production or service, sagging sales, ill health and poor attendance of employees, and lack of communication, spirit, and collaboration. Some common and persistent dysfunctional patterns include idealistic vision taking precedence over real and immediate human considerations, group trance (in which we "drink the Kool-Aid" without deeply questioning what we are doing), shaming and blaming, avoidance, gossip, unconscious expressions of rank and power, discrimination, low energy and apathy, and disconnection between words and actions.

In all cases, individual and group awareness, dialogue, and purposeful effort can transform missing pieces into fuel for growth and development. These pieces often serve as the edges of growth; they are issues that indicate opportunities for increased awareness and self-development. We can even use them to "engineer breakdowns," in the words of Tim Murphy of Growth River Consulting, a firm that focuses on facilitating multi-stakeholder problem-solving, in order to accelerate learning and growth. Breaking through our holes, blocks, and shadows creates movement, flow, and even ecstasy: experiencing ourselves as discrete beings moving as part of a unified whole, with lightness, joy, and energy. This experience is available to us in every moment, and we can touch it every time we move through our missing pieces.

EXPERIENCING INTERDEPENDENCE

When you tug at a single thing in nature, you find it attached to the rest of the world.

—JOHN MUIR

When we "just do one thing," we are always doing more than that, since no one thing exists unto itself, separate from all else. Embracing this principle fosters awareness of complexity, sensitivity to relationships, and thoughtful action. Awareness of the interdependent nature of phenomena fosters actions that anticipate system effects, unintended consequences, and emergent opportunities.

By considering interdependence in the design and development of our businesses, we can purposefully build an intricate web of relationships, recognizing the meaningful role all parts play, distributing responsibility, authority, and accountability, and considering and addressing the needs, interests, and perspectives of all stakeholders.

When we encounter stubborn obstacles, we can settle into interdependence and see new pathways to explore for solutions. If parts of our business ecosystem do not seem ready to grow or develop, we can focus on other parts until we find what is ready to move next, knowing that when any part moves, so does the whole system. When no single part moves, we recognize the opportunity to address the whole system, or combinations of parts or stakeholders. And if we identify unaddressed issues, we can work on them at any level of the system (ourselves, relationships, or stakeholder relations) and influence the entire system along the way.

Interdependence is also relevant to Working for Good, as it integrates our work life with the rest of our life, to create a whole life. Play, rest, intimacy, meaning, purpose, and passion belong in every aspect of life; and if we bring them to work, work is enlivened and life flows.

Exercise: Experiencing Interdependence

Sit or stand comfortably. If you are standing, bend your knees slightly. Take a few deep breaths. Feel your jaw and your shoulders drop as gravity does its work. With each inhale, feel your spine lengthen. With each exhale, feel your shoulders and jaw surrender to gravity. Scan your body to sense whether there is any tension. If you find some, breathe into it and observe it. Then move on.

Reflect back to the clear mountain lake representing awareness that we envisioned at the beginning of this book. See and feel that lake, and note any sensations, feelings, thoughts, or insights that come up for you as you visualize the lake.

Now see a small stream running from the lake down the mountainside. And see this stream gradually pick up speed and size as it gathers water from the mountain and becomes a river—the river of embodiment—touching your passion, intentions, purpose, principles, and commitments. Observe and feel the river gaining momentum and force.

Now see the river converging with another, representing the other, in a process of connection. Feel the merging. Create space with your breath—expanding as you inhale, letting go of your thoughts and feelings as you exhale; open to the other without judgment, with patience and interest. And feel the two rivers become one.

Now see this river meet several others and merge in true collaboration to create a powerful, purposeful river raging toward the sea.

And see it reach the sea, expanding into the open space, feeling simultaneously connected and expansive. Experience the water.

As you continue to breathe, feel the water evaporating into the sky and moving in a warm, steady breeze back up the course of the river to the stream, to the lake. And feel it meeting a cold breeze from the other direction, as water condenses, clouds form, and rain falls into the lake. And feel the cycle continue: the lake feeds the stream, which becomes a river, and the flow continues.

When you are ready, take a few deep breaths, and relax.

Business in the World of Stakeholders

Like an organism or an ecosystem in nature, a business is a living system, not a machine, and we are among its constituents—as owners, customers, team members, community members, vendors. The way we embody these roles and engage with businesses informs the nature of business itself.

As the authors of the 1999 treatise *The Cluetrain Manifesto* observed, "Markets are conversations," not monologues from companies to consumers, and the new social media technologies are facilitating global networks of informed and empowered consumers and employees. Companies are no longer the sole or even principal generators of ideas and information relating to their own businesses. "People in networked markets have figured out that they get far better information and support from one another than from vendors. So much for corporate rhetoric about adding value to commoditized products. There are no secrets. The networked market knows more than companies do about their own products. And whether the news is good or bad, they tell everyone."

Another reflection of the organic stakeholder system is the powerful phenomenon known as "crowd sourcing," which catalyzes the wisdom of groups to inform decisions. In *We Are Smarter Than Me*, Barry Liebert and Jon Spector tell the stories of dozens of businesses—from large corporations like Proctor & Gamble, Eli Lilly, IBM, and Virgin Mobile to smaller companies like Australian brewery Brewtopia—that are designing their products, creating marketing campaigns, and delivering customer service by tapping into large groups of people online, around the world. Crowd sourcing deepens the interconnectedness between stakeholders and illuminates that we exist in a complex, interdependent relationship with business.

This network effect is happening in other ways too. Leslie Crutchfield and Heather McLeod Grant outline the six practices of high-impact nonprofits in their book *Force for Good*, based on years of thorough research and analysis. One practice is "nurturing nonprofit networks" to collaborate with aligned organizations and advance the larger field they work in. In my work facilitating multisector alliances, I find increasing openness to collaboration between diverse groups and recognition of the essential need for such cross-sector and multiple-stakeholder collaborations to address social issues while advancing individual interests. By purposefully serving the whole, we serve ourselves, and we can design our business ecosystems to serve both.

Marketing as Integration

Marketing is like skin: it connects the inner business with the marketplace. To continue the metaphor, marketing covers the entire spectrum of a business. By representing and communicating what a business stands for and what it sells, marketing calls on everyone within it and every communication emanating from it to be clear, connected, and true to the essence and identity of the company. Like skin, marketing serves an integrative function, holding a company together and reflecting its integrity. It provides the platform for resonance, attracts outside stakeholders—investors, customers, new team members—and cultivates sustainable, ongoing relationships with them.

One of my mentors, creative publicist Terry Randolph, taught me this: "The thing you are promoting is the promotion." That is, your marketing strategies and tactics emanate from what it is you are promoting; understand it and the aspects of it that your audience connects with, and there is the source of your promotion. In some ways this is similar to Process Work (call it process marketing): find the signal where there is energy and amplify it—bring it to life in ways that are larger than life. For example, Terry and I worked together to promote the musician Yanni, who held concerts at World Heritage Sites like the Taj Mahal, the Forbidden City, and the Acropolis, reflecting the epic, romantic nature of his music on the largest scale imaginable.

MEASURING SUCCESS

Success is the ability to create happiness for others.
—MARCELLA ECHAVARRIA

Remember Ed Freeman's analogy: "We need red blood cells to live (the same way a business needs profits to live), but the purpose of life is not to make red blood cells (the same way the purpose of business is not to exist to make profits)." The same way we count red blood cells to ensure that we are healthy, we need to count money—with integrity and clarity—to make certain our businesses are healthy and sustainable.

Just as we don't measure a person's life, overall health, and well-being in red blood cells—happiness, peace of mind, vitality, productivity, and joy cannot be measured that way—we cannot determine the ultimate health of a business solely by counting money. We must also count the other things we value. You value what you count, so count what you value. If you value a healthy business culture, count team-member turnover, absenteeism, and performance. If you value long-term relationships, count investor longevity and customer loyalty. If you value the environment, count your company's positive and negative environmental impact. If you value balance and overall health and well-being, then count vacations, continuing education, community service, family time, and other activities that build well-rounded lives for you, your colleagues, and your coworkers.

When you count, use objective measures to the greatest extent you can. Set criteria and follow them. Elicit feedback from all stakeholders and engage them in addressing the issues and challenges that arise.

SUE'S UNFOLDING PATH: MASTERY THROUGH PRACTICE

We fail to realize that mastery is not about perfection. It's about a process, a journey. The master is the one who stays on the path day after day, year after year. The master is the one who is willing to try, and fail, and try again, for as long as he or she lives.

—GEORGE LEONARD, in *Mastery*

Grounded in her passion, purpose, and principles, supported by a deepening awareness practice, and manifesting through a healthy collaborative process, Sue continues to develop and implement the YEP! program. She understands her role as a facilitative leader and recognizes the importance of the ongoing cultivation of her skills of awareness, embodiment, connection, collaboration, and integration. She engages talented mentors and colleagues to support her learning and growth.

Sue focuses much of her efforts on bringing out the best—activating passion, purpose, creativity, and initiative—in her clients (the students), and her colleagues and coworkers. She increasingly learns to be present to the moment and respond to people and circumstances for what they are, not the stories she carries about them.

Sue finds that the more she serves others, the greater the results she sees in the overall program and the more success and recognition YEP! experiences as a business, as the combined and aligned energy and enthusiasm of all involved create a powerful, dynamic force. She recognizes that the art of facilitation really does make things easier, as she leverages her time and talent by supporting others to excel in their work.

Mastery is a process, not a destination. Rather than presuming to be a master, we continually aspire to mastery and practice our skills to continually elevate our adeptness.

Imitating masters is not mastery, but learning from masters can enhance our progress toward it. Mentors can play a significant role in advancing our knowledge and understanding, providing us with encouragement, appropriate challenges, and honest reflection that supports our process. We can learn from our colleagues, and even from our competitors. The ancient Greeks pursued *arête*—a state of excellence cultivated through practice and competition. In this sense, competition is not about winning and losing but about striving for excellence, and as we achieve new levels of mastery we inspire our competitors to new levels of excellence, which, in turn, drives us ever higher.

Recognizing that mastery is a process rather than a destination deepens humility and drives ongoing learning and development. As we stretch ourselves and each other, we realize more of our potential, expand our capacity, and invigorate our lives.

PUTTING THE PRACTICES TO WORK

That which we persist in doing becomes easier for us to do. Not that the nature of the thing itself has changed but our power to do it is increased.
—RALPH WALDO EMERSON

I opened this book by acknowledging that I like to work. I also love practice. There is something about moving into a place that tests, stretches, and transforms me that I find extremely appealing, even if sometimes exhausting. And when the "thing gets easier," it creates the opportunity to try a new thing or to cultivate it at a higher level.

About thirty years ago I identified my purpose: leveraging the power of business to foster personal growth and social transformation, for the greater good.

Among my core principles are:

1. The process is the product.
2. Growth is imperative.
3. Cultivate love and compassion.

4. Embrace change and diversity.

5. Respect the individual and understand the interdependent whole.

6. Keep moving and find delight in stillness.

7. Dance with the emergent, unfolding reality.

My talents include the ability to envision and activate, lead, collaborate, and facilitate, fulfill my commitments, and bring out the best in others. My passion is to use my talent to fulfill my purpose. My principal intention and commitment is to fulfill my purpose while embodying my principles.

Adding this all up has led me to where I am today, heading up FLOW, writing this book, and catalyzing Cause Alliance Marketing programs, including Conscious Capitalism®, Peace Through Commerce®, and Accelerating Women Entrepreneurs™ through FLOW—and, in collaboration with others, the Optimal Health Alliance.

The Cause Alliance Marketing programs deeply reflect the principle of integration. Organizational partners bring their assets, resources, and capabilities together to collaboratively address a shared social purpose, while simultaneously addressing their respective needs and objectives.

Writing this book has been another exercise in integration, affording me the opportunity and motivation to focus intensely on the lessons I have learned during the past thirty years and the skills I apply to support that learning and the ongoing realization of my purpose. Deeply engaged in the ongoing work of facilitating alliances, building programs, and producing events, the process of focusing and representing my insights provides an incredible feedback loop, deepening and accelerating my practice of Working for Good. And the way I produced the book, in collaboration with others, reflects and reinforces the principles of collaboration and integration.

I employ a repertoire of practices to reinforce integration and the overall process of Working for Good, including the personal practices of mindfulness meditation, yoga, 5Rhythms moving meditation practice, ChiRunning, body surfing, and some martial arts. In case it is not apparent, the bodily/kinesthetic channel is one of my principal ways of relating to the world. Other practices I employ include responding to most emails within twenty-four hours, writing monthly reflections, maintaining a daily agenda to support me in fulfilling my commitments—and, if I cannot fulfill an explicit commitment, to let others involved know that I cannot do so, so they can adjust accordingly. Another is to recite basic intentions and commitments with respect to my personal conduct every morning to tune me in to the way I want to be in the world.

To a significant extent, I select my projects and develop programs by considering how they tie in with the other programs I am facilitating and other things I am doing. And, finally—and it takes time to get it, at least it has for me—I have established a sustainable balance between work and the rest of life, with lots of play and playfulness running through both.

If Goethe is right, saying yes to what we want to create within ourselves calls forth forces to help us become what we commit to becoming.

> **Writing Reflection:** What Is Your Integration Story?
> Have a pen and notebook handy. Take a few deep breaths and surrender your jaw and shoulders to gravity. Scan your body for any tension, and breath into it, releasing it as you exhale.

Reflect on the following questions.

What are your passion and purpose? What principles guide you in your work? What are your intentions and commitments with respect to your work?

_____

_____

_____

How does your work currently reflect these?

_____

_____

_____

To what extent do you cultivate awareness and practice the skills of connection, collaboration, and integration?

_____

_____

What is the relationship between your work life and the rest of your life?

_____

_____

_____

_____

What are your growing edges—the places in you that need the light of awareness, support, and practice to transform and integrate?

_____

_____

_____

What other reflections do you have on your story?

_____

_____

_____

_____

SUMMARY: INTEGRATION—RECOMMENDATIONS FOR ACTION

Hell, there are no rules here. We're trying to accomplish something.

—THOMAS EDISON

A couple of days before I wrote this section, I had an interview with my friend and colleague Chris White, whose company, Good, Gold, Global, focuses on globalization for good. Among other things, Chris asked me about the journey that led to doing what I do, and he closed by asking if I had any advice to pass on to young people who want to Work for Good. My response to Chris was, essentially, to train your mind: meditate or cultivate another practice that quiets your mind, gives you perspective on it, and frees you from the shackles of cultural conditioning and other baggage that inhibits your being present without judgment. Learn to listen, and do it fully, deeply, and without preconceptions and prejudices. Keep your word. Fulfill your commitments, and when you can't, be open and explicit: say you will not be able to and make appropriate adjustments.

To this I now add: Care for your body, mind, emotions, and spirit. Feed your strengths, cultivate your intelligence, fuel your passion, pursue your purpose, intensify your intentions, affirm your principles, deepen your commitments, and practice all five skills of Working for Good in an integrated and balanced way. Find good mentors, friends, and colleagues, and serve people well.

Writing Reflection: Activating Your Integration Story

Tune in again and reflect on the following questions:

What are your next steps, the things you are going to do to activate and sustain your integration story and your process of Working for Good?

_____

_____

_____

_____

_____

What are you going to do with respect to:
Taking care of yourself?

_____

_____

_____

_____

_____

_____

Taking care of others?

_____

_____

_____

Developing the skills of awareness, embodiment, connection, collaboration, and integration?

_____

_____

Defining your passion, intentions, purpose, principles, and commitments?

_____

_____

_____

_____

Identifying and engaging others—e.g., collaborators and mentors?

_____

_____

_____

_____

Allocating time and resources to support your process?

_____

_____

Chapter Seven

RETURN

*We must not cease from exploration. And the end
of all our exploring will be to arrive where we began
and to know the place for the first time.*

—T. S. ELIOT

In his extensive studies of the mythologies of the cultures of the world, Joseph Campbell discovered and described the archetypal hero's journey. The journey begins with the Call, when the hero heeds the call to pursue a compelling purpose. He leaves the familiar world he knows to venture into the unknown, risking comfort, safety, social standing—essentially everything—in the process. In the next stage of the journey, Descent, the hero descends into the underworld. Here he is forced to let go of what he knew and did in the past; here also, he encounters naysayers and other obstacles to his journey. In the next stage, Travels Through the Underworld, he faces his greatest fears, is tempted by forces that will pull him off his pursuit of his purpose, and finally meets allies who bestow upon him the powerful tools he needs to support him through the journey.

Ultimately, after surviving a symbolic death in order to find what he was looking for on the journey, the hero re-emerges in the final stage, Return. Though the hero wants to enjoy the fruits of his labor and bask in the warm light of success, the power of his purpose and his commitment to his community lead him back to the normal, everyday world he once inhabited. However, he returns transformed, bringing with him the gifts he picked up on his journey to share them with the rest of humanity—gifts of experience, insight, wisdom, and the will to serve others and spread love and joy. This return is not a turning back, but a moving through—through the challenges, obstacles, and lessons of the journey. It means letting go of the temptation to hold on to limiting thoughts and ways of being and doing, and overcoming the fears, distractions, and delusions that threaten to steer us off course or convince us that we have already arrived at our destination when we have hardly begun the journey.

The journey into Working for Good is very much a hero's journey, filled with risks, challenges, allies, and transformational experiences. It takes tenacity, persistence, perseverance, resilience, optimism, faith, keen awareness, and powerful tools to fulfill our purpose. And even upon our return, we continue to face adversity, obstacles, naysayers, and challenges, both internal and external.

Just as the hero finds allies on his journey through the underworld, we find mentors to guide us and support us in finding strength and skill within ourselves. As the Buddha advised students and seekers to find *sangha,* or like-minded community, to support them in their cultivation of insight, wisdom, and love, similarly, we attract and convene our community of like-minded conscious entrepreneurs and change agents who are committed to cultivating the skills of Working for Good and to serving others through their work.

All along, we grow and learn through the skills of awareness, embodiment, connection, collaboration, and integration—each of which supports us as we learn, grow, and sustain ourselves on the journey.

Exercise: Lovingkindness Meditation

Just as connecting with love is one of the fruits of the journey, we can use the power of love as an antidote to doubt, resentment, and other undermining emotions triggered by our own insecurities and the challenges from others.

Sit or stand comfortably. If you are standing, bend your knees slightly. Take a few deep breaths. Feel your jaw and your shoulders drop as gravity does its work. With each inhale feel your spine lengthen. With each exhale feel your shoulders and jaw surrender to gravity. Scan your body to sense if there is any tension. If you find any, breathe into it, and observe it. Then move on.

Focus your attention on your heart or heart center. As you inhale, feel it fill up, as a balloon fills up with air. As you exhale, feel it soften, relax, and radiate outward.

Picture—in your mind and heart—someone you love dearly. It can be a child, your spouse, a parent, anyone who is easy for you to express your love to and for. Feel them in your heart, and feel yourself extending your love to them, sending them wishes for happiness, health, and well-being.

When you are ready, shift your attention to someone you like and respect very much who is easy for you to be with and express yourself with. As you continue to breathe evenly and deeply, feel them in your heart and feel yourself extending your love to them, sending them wishes for happiness, health, and well-being.

Again, when you are ready, shift again. This time, to someone you know, but perhaps not all that well or, even if you know them well, you don't have strong feelings about them. Feel this person in your heart, and feel yourself extending your love to them, sending them wishes for happiness, health, and well-being.

Now shift to someone who is difficult for you, perhaps someone you work with whom you don't get along with. As you continue to breathe evenly and deeply, feel them in your heart, and feel yourself extending your love to them, sending them wishes for happiness, health, and well-being.

When you are ready, shift your attention to yourself. As you continue to breathe evenly and deeply, feel yourself and feel love filling your being as you radiate with happiness, health, and well-being.

While you continue to feel yourself, extend your love to the others again, and beyond them to everyone you know, and everyone you don't know—opening yourself to love and to your ability to express it, and receive it.

When you are ready, bow to yourself, and move on—carrying the knowledge and the experience of love and of Working for Good, and cultivating both as you go.

The more I practice the skills of Working for Good, while carrying the intention to serve through my work, the more I relate to an insight by Mother Teresa:

> *I never look at the masses as my responsibility; I look at the individual. I can only love one person at a time—just one, one, one. So you begin. I began—I picked up one person. Maybe if I didn't pick up that one person, I wouldn't have picked up forty-two thousand. . . . The same thing goes for you, the same thing in your family, the same thing in your church, your community. Just begin—one, one, one.*

Working for Good is essentially about how we show up for one person at a time, and for each person we encounter. There is no "saving the world," but there is co-creating it with one another. To do that, we have to truly be with one another.

RECIPROCITY

> *You cannot hold on to anything good. You must be continually giving—and getting. You cannot hold on to your seed. You must sow it—and reap anew. You cannot hold onto riches. You must use them and get other riches in return.*
>
> —ROBERT COLLIER

Nature has a wonderful and mysterious way of fostering dynamic equilibrium: balance that is off-balance. Give and take, up and down, never static, always moving from life into death into life into death, and so on. Cycles and spirals, with dynamic exchange between individuals, groups, and systems. The marketplace is a wonderful metaphor for the functioning of nature, and a powerful tool for driving individual growth, societal development, and the evolution of humanity. The principle of voluntary exchange underlying the marketplace promotes freedom, creativity, and service. And it highlights the essential roles of giving and receiving in nature, in business, and in life. In the words of John Lennon and Paul McCartney, "the love you take is equal to the love you make." While "equal" in this context does not have to be taken literally, Working for Good invites us to approach our work with the intention to give and serve, but also to be open to receiving, in order to sustain our work and deepen our ability to serve even more powerfully. This is not a martyr's path, but a gateway to joy and abundance.

Writing Reflection: Resolution

One who makes a resolution and then makes sincere efforts to realize her dreams, nothing stops her from realizing her goal.

—RIG VEDA

Take a few deep breaths, tune in, and reflect on the following questions:

What is the gift or gifts that you are bringing back with you from your journey through this book?

_____

_____

_____

_____

What will you do with these gifts?

_____

_____

_____

What are the first things you will do, and when will you do them?

_____

_____

_____

_____

I encourage you to get out your calendar or agenda, and use it to map out your next steps. And remember to reach out to mentors, advisors, and peers for guidance and support, and to return to the place within yourself where you connect with the passion, sense of purpose, awareness, and energy to sustain you on your journey.

A bit of advice given to a young Native American at the time of his initiation: "As you go the way of life, you will see a great chasm. Jump. It's not as wide as you think."

—JOSEPH CAMPBELL

A REMINDER ABOUT THE EXERCISES

I encourage you to practice the exercises in this book frequently to support you to cultivate the skills of Working for Good.

Remember that you can practice the exercises as you are reading them. You can read them, then practice them. You can have someone else read them to you while you practice them. Or, you can go to workingforgood.com/exercises, select this exercise, hit "play," and we will talk you through the exercise.

While you are at workingforgood.com, you can also sign up for my monthly newsletter, find out about Working for Good workshops, and access other Working for Good resources.

ACKNOWLEDGMENTS

Gratitude is not only the greatest of virtues,
but the parent of all the others.

—CICERO

I am grateful to all who have inspired and taught me along my path of *Working for Good,* all who have supported me in the process of writing this book, and to you, for aspiring to be Working for Good, and for making it this far in your journey.

Specifically, I am grateful to Elad Levinson and Julie van Amerongen, my friends, colleagues, and collaborators on this book. Their steadfast presence, thoughtful reflections, and loving support were essential to my process of writing this book and gave me the opportunity to deepen my embodiment of the principles of *Working for Good.*

I am deeply grateful to Tami Simon, founder and publisher of Sounds True, for recognizing the truth in *Working for Good* and for inviting me to publish with Sounds True. In addition to saying "yes" to the book, my editor, Kelly Notaras, gave me a life-changing gift when she responded to the first draft I submitted—kindly ripping it to shreds, while pointing out all of the jewels among the rubble, and, in the process, helping me to find my authentic voice as an author. I am especially grateful to and impressed by the Sounds True marketing, design, and administration team, whose support and collaborative spirit I have felt from day one. I would specifically like to thank Chantal Pierrat, Shelly Vickroy, Beverly Yates, and Jaime Schwalb.

Early in the process of writing this book I interviewed about a dozen friends and colleagues. Their insights, energy, and enthusiasm inspired, informed, and validated much of my experience and understandings. So, thank you to Anne Marie Burgoyne, Magatte Wade, Mark Albion, Chris White, Cheryl Fields Tyler, Yasuhiko Kimura, Robb Smith, Marcella Echavarria, Richard Spiegel, C. J. Hayden, Traci Fenton, Sam Rosen, and Nickolas Knightly for your time and thoughtful attention, and for the great work you do.

Special thanks to John Mackey and Michael Strong, co-founders of FLOW, and my colleagues and collaborators in building FLOW from an idea into an emerging movement. Your penetrating brilliance, illuminating insights, passionate commitment to doing good, and playful spirits delight and inspire me daily. And thanks to the FLOW board, Susan Niederhoffer, Vidar Jorgensen, Jim von Ehr, and Randy Eisenman for supporting me to write this book while serving as executive director and chief activation officer for FLOW.

A deep bow of acknowledgment and appreciation to my friend and colleague Phyllis Blees, VP and Chief Problem Solver for FLOW, who exemplifies the spirit of Working for Good, carrying deep commitment to liberate the entrepreneurial spirit for good, serving others, and making the world a better place through innovative, ethical, and responsible business. Her ferocious loyalty to colleagues and company, impeccable attention to detail, and great care for people and property inspire me daily.

Thank you to Kartar Singh Khalsa, CEO of Golden Temple of Oregon, for engaging me to produce the Celebrate Peace program for Peace Cereal, which gave birth to the name Working for Good and focused me on articulating what it means to me.

Another deep bow of appreciation to George Morgan, German Perez, the late Robert Rodale, Peter Baumann, Greg Pardes, Brando Crespi, Terry Randolph, Larry Pentoney, Tom White, Kenny Ausubel and Nina Simon, Katherine and Danny Dreyer, Johnny G, Yanni, Stephen and Leyla Hill, Jack Kornfield, Jim Root, Margaret Jane, Christiana Wyly, and the countless other collaborators and teachers who have helped me to define my path and practice of Working for Good.

Special thanks to my parents Mark and Patty Klein, whose love, support, and guidance set me on my path of Working for Good and whose questions, challenges, and encouragement continue to support my growth and development. My siblings, Steve, Jim, and Gail were the first guinea pigs for my nascent leadership and facilitation skills, which, at the beginning, were undoubtedly as subtle as a cave man's club at times. Thank you for your love, patience, and persistent presence in my life. It is through my family that I have learned the lessons of trust, steadfastness, and love. I am forever grateful, and I love you all very much.

Toward the end of her life of ninety-nine years, my grandmother Nettie Finkle played a special role for me, helping me to reconcile my relationship to money and to her late husband, my grandfather David Finkle among other things. Your spirit and guidance will continue to influence and support me, Gram. Thank you.

Thank you Jacqueline, whose playful loving spirit supported me down the home stretch of writing this book, and whose recognition of the merit of this work touched me deeply.

Finally but certainly not last, my deepest appreciation to my daughter Meryl Fé. If I ever needed a reason to focus on Working for Good and to make a positive difference in the world, you are certainly that reason. Being your father is the most challenging and rewarding job I have ever taken on, and it provides the greatest returns. May you always be healthy and happy, and may you find your own path to Working for Good. I love you.

NOTES

1   Well known as a parable, this story appears on many Web sites. It appears in *Zen Flesh, Zen Bones: A Collection of Zen and Pre-Zen Writings* Compiled by Paul Reps and Nyogen Senzaki (Boston: Shambhala, 1994) and *Peace Tales: World Folktales to Talk About* by Margaret Read MacDonald (North Haven, CT: Linnet Books, 1992). This story appears on numerous Web sites and in several other books. Master Bankei was a Japanese Zen master who lived from 1622 to 1693.

2   Paraphrased from *Zen Shorts* by John J. Muth (New York: Longitude, 2005).

3   From Chade-Meng Tan's Website, "What Do You Think, My Friend?" serve.com/~cmtan/buddhism/Lighter/shortstories.html

4   From *The Happiness Solution: Finding Joy and Meaning in an Upside Down World* by Alan Gettis (Bloomington, IN: Trafford Publishing, 2006).

5   A story told by Jack Kornfield that can be found at serve.com/~cmtan/buddhism/lighter/shortstories.html.

ADDITIONAL RESOURCES

As in any journey, it helps to have support and good resources to travel the path of Working for Good. Peer groups, mentors, and other real-time human support is essential and ideal. Media resources, courses, and workshops can also be powerful tools to support your journey.

Here are some of the resources I have learned from and drawn upon during my journey. I continue to consult many of them for support along the way. I have organized them as "General Resources," and resources related to each of the chapters that correspond to the skills of Working for Good. Some resources transcend a single category and therefore appear in more than one.

GENERAL RESOURCES

One of the most dependable sources of insight and guidance for me is Stephen Mitchell's translation of the *Tao Te Ching* (New York: Harper Perennial Modern Classics, 2006), the Chinese classic written by Lao Tzu around the sixth century BC.

I recommend two new resources by my friends and colleagues at FLOW, which help to set and deepen the context for Conscious Capitalism and the power of entrepreneurship and market-based solutions to global challenges and opportunities. They are *Passion and Purpose: The Power of Conscious Capitalism* (Boulder, CO: Sounds True, 2009), a two-CD set with John Mackey, and *Be the Solution: How Entrepreneurs and Conscious Capitalists Can Solve All the World's Problems* by Michael Strong (Hoboken, NJ: John Wiley & Sons, 2009). Brian Johnson's *PhilosophersNotes* (available at PhilosophersNotes.com) are an excellent source of time-less and contemporary wisdom from thought leaders in many fields, with great relevance to all aspects of Working for Good.

Other excellent books that illuminate the transformational power of business and the emerging new business paradigm are *Firms of Endearment* by David Wolfe, Raj Sisodia, and Jag Sheth; (Upper Saddle River, NJ: Wharton School Publishing, 2006.) *Megatrends 2010: The Rise of Conscious Capitalism* by Patricia Aburdene (Charlottesville, VA: Hampton Roads Publishing Company, 2007); *Conscious Business* by Fred Kofman (Boulder: Sounds True, 2006); *Creating a World Without Poverty* by Muhammad Yunus (New York: PublicAffairs, 2007); and *Good Business* (New York: The Penguin Group, 2003) by Mihaly Csikszentmihalyi, author of *Flow: The Psychology of Optimal Experience* (New York: Harper Perennial, 1991). Daniel Pink's *A Whole New Mind* (New York: The Penguin Group, 2005) celebrates the rise of right-brain thinking and the qualities associated with it in business; *Forces for Good* by Leslie Crutchfield and Heather McLeod Grant (New York: The Penguin Group, 2005) presents the qualities of high-performing nonprofits; and *We Are Smarter Than Me* by Barry Libert and Jon Spector (Upper Saddle River, NJ: Wharton School Publishing, 2008) elucidates the power of crowd-sourcing—engaging large groups to inform business processes and decisions.

In his bestselling book *The Tipping Point: How Little Things Can Make a Big Difference* (New York: Little, Brown and Company, 2000), Malcolm Gladwell describes the processes behind dramatic transformations and the mysterious phenomena that lead to hit products, major social changes, and the spread of new ideas. *ODE* and *GOOD* magazines are wonderful contemporary chronicles of emerging new realities, with a positive and optimistic orientation, interesting stories, and excellent writing.

AWARENESS

American Buddhist meditation teacher Jack Kornfield is both a masterful teacher and an excellent writer. His books—which include *A Path with Heart* (New York: Bantam Books, 1993); *After the Ecstasy, the Laundry* (New York: Bantam Books, 2000); *Stories of the Spirit, Stories of the Heart* (New York: HarperCollins, 1991) and more—are superb guides to the inner experience of mindfulness. Vietnamese Zen Buddhist master Thich Nhat Hanh's books are like a master calligrapher's painting—clear, crisp, illuminating, and stunningly beautiful.

To deepen your understanding of multiple intelligences, check out *Frames of Mind: The Theory of Multiple Intelligences* by Howard Gardener (New York: Basic Books, 1993). And for more on emotional intelligence, look at Daniel Goleman's *Working with Emotional Intelligence* (New York: Bantam Books, 1998) and *Primal Leadership: Realizing the Power of Emotional Intelligence* (Cambridge, MA: Harvard Business School Publishing, 2002).

Viktor Frankl's *Man's Search for Meaning* (Boston: Beacon Press, 2006) and Martin Seligman's *Authentic Happiness: A New*

Approach to Psychology (New York: The Free Press, 2002) shed bright light on the power of our minds and choices to make a difference in our lives. Dr. Seligman's "Authentic Happiness" website has many great resources for exploring your relationship to happiness: authentichappiness.sas.upenn.edu.

All of Arnold Mindell's books are about cultivating awareness and applying it in different contexts. I especially like *The Leader as Martial Artist* (San Francisco: Harper, 1992), *Sitting in the Fire* (Portland, OR: Lao Tse, 1995) and *The Shaman's Body* (New York: HarperCollins, 1993).

EMBODIMENT

ChiRunning (New York: Fireside/Simon & Schuster, 2004) and *ChiWalking* (New York: Fireside/Simon & Schuster, Inc., 2006) by Danny and Katherine Dreyer, and Gabrielle Roth's books, especially *Maps to Ecstasy* (Novato, CA: New World Library, 1998), provide great tools for bringing awareness into your body and embodying awareness in movement. Classes and practice in ChiRunning, ChiWalking, and 5Rhythms moving meditation practice provide great support for bringing embodied awareness to work.

I also love yoga in general and kundalini yoga in particular as tools for cultivating embodied awareness. *Integral Life Practice: A Twenty-First Century Blueprint for Physical Health, Emotional Balance, Mental Clarity, and Spiritual Awakening* by Ken Wilber et al. (Boston: Integral Books, 2008) is a comprehensive guide to embodying an integral worldview in everyday life.

Buddha 9 to 5 by Nancy Spears (Avon, MA: Adams Media, 2007) is an excellent guide to applying the principles and practices of Buddhism to business.

James Hillman's *The Soul's Code* (New York: Warner Books, 1996) is a profoundly inspiring book that encourages us to trust in the unfolding of our unique path and to discover our singular purpose. Hillman's book *Kinds of Power* (New York: Currency Doubleday, 1995) provides great insight into power and the different ways we can cultivate, express, and exercise it.

In *The Element: How Finding Your Passion Changes Everything*, (New York: Viking, 2009) Sir Ken Robinson explores the powerful convergence of talent and passion to release creative expression and well-being.

Authentic Leadership: Rediscovering the Secrets to Creating Lasting Value (San Francisco: Jossey-Bass, 2003) and *True North: Discover Your Authentic Leadership* (San Francisco: Jossey-Bass, 2007) by Bill George are excellent guides to embodying authentic leadership.

Purpose is a significant aspect of Working for Good and the subject of a host of excellent books. *It's Not What You Sell, It's What You Stand For* by Roy Spence Jr. and Haley Rushing (New York: The Penguin Group, 2009) is both inspiring and practical. *Purpose: The Starting Point of Great Companies* by Nikos Mourkogiannis (New York: Palgrave MacMillan, 2006) is the deeply researched and thoughtful exploration of purpose, with excellent examples of purpose-driven entrepreneurs and businesses. Christine Arena's *The High-Purpose Company* (New York: HarperCollins, 2007) is also meticulously researched and superbly written.

Mark Albion, cofounder of NetImpact, a network of socially-minded MBA students, and a pioneer in the realm of social business, has authored several inspiring and informative books, including *Making a Life, Making a*

Living: Reclaiming Your Purpose and Passion in Business and in Life (New York: Warner Books, 2000) and *True to Yourself: Leading a Values-Based Business* (San Francisco: Berrett-Koehler Publishers, 2006).

Stephen Covey's *The Seven Habits of Highly Effective People* (New York: Simon and Schuster, 1989) is a timeless classic packed with inspiring insights and great lessons.

Raising the Bar: The Story of Clif Bar by Gary Erickson (San Francisco: Jossey-Bass, 2004) is an inspiring story about sticking to principles.

While their focus is on martial combat, the Chinese classic *The Art of War* (London: Oxford Press, 1963) and the Japanese classic *A Book of Five Rings* (Woodstock, NY: Overlook Press, 1974) provide great insights into principles and mastery.

CONNECTION

Thomas Moore's *Care of the Soul* (New York: HarperCollins, 1992) and *A Life at Work* (New York: Broadway Books, 2008) touch on the deeper dimensions of being within doing.

How to Listen So Kids Will Listen and *Listen So Kids Will Talk* by Adele Faber and Elaine Mazlish (New York: Avon Books, 1980) should be required reading for everyone, parent or not.

Rules of the Dialogue Game by Peter Winchell (San Rafael, CA: The Invisible Press, 2009) is a great, practical guide to cultivating the practice of dialogue. *The Way of Council* by Jack Zimmerman and Virginia Coyle (Las Vegas: Bramble Books, 1996) is a practical guide to the practice of council.

Strunk and White's eighty-five-page classic *The Elements of Style* (Ithaca, NY: BN Publishing, 2006) is up there with the *Tao Te Ching* as the biggest small book ever written. It is an essential guide to cultivating conscious and effective writing and to use of the English language in general. *The Artist's Way: A Spiritual Path to Higher Creativity* by Julia Cameron (New York: Penguin Putnam: 2002) is one of my collaborator Julie van Amerongen's all-time favorites. *Writing Down the Bones* by Natalie Goldberg (Boston: Shambhala, 1986) is another classic about writing as practice.

As tools for connecting, I highly recommend *Nonviolent Communication: A Language of Life* by Marshall B. Rosenberg and Arun Gandhi (Encinitas, CA: Puddle Dancer Press, 2003) and *Appreciative Inquiry: A Positive Revolution in Change* by David L. Cooperrider and Diana Whitney (San Francisco: Berrett-Koehler Publishers, 2005).

Adrian Chan's Gravity7.com has excellent resources for understanding the way people relate through the new social media and for learning how to connect with people using social media.

COLLABORATION

Interaction Associates provides superb training in facilitating collaboration and facilitative leadership; visit them at interactionassociates.com. I also recommend IA cofounder David Straus's excellent book *How to Make Collaboration Work: Powerful Ways to Build Consensus, Solve Problems, and Make Decisions* (San Francisco: Berrett-Koehler, 2002).

Presence by Peter Senge et al. (New York: Doubleday, 2004) sets out a system and process for cultivating presence and facilitating organizational transformation through inner work and collaboration. *Getting to Yes: Negotiating Agreement Without Giving In* by Roger Fisher and William Ury (New

York: Houghton Mifflin, 1991) provides simple, straight-forward, and profoundly useful insights into the process of effectively negotiating from principle in order to foster mutually beneficial outcomes.

Akira Kurosawa's *Seven Samurai* is my favorite movie of all time, principally because of its utter mastery of the presentation of archetypal human character—i.e., what human beings are like and what they do. It is a great story of collaboration.

All of the resources that cultivate awareness also support collaboration. In particular, Arnold Mindell's *The Leader As Martial Artist* is profoundly useful in the context of facilitating collaboration. Stephen Covey's *Seven Habits of Highly Effective Families* (New York: Golden Books, 1997) and *Principle-Centered Leadership* (New York: Fireside, 1990) are excellent.

INTEGRATION

The Fifth Discipline (New York: Doubleday, 1990) and *The Fifth Discipline Fieldbook* by Peter Senge et al. (New York: Currency/Doubleday, 1994) are superb guides to cultivating systems thinking and an integrated array of practices to foster integration.

While it applies specifically to building design and community planning, *A Pattern Language* by Christopher Alexander et al. (New York: Oxford University Press, 1977) is an incredible tool for cultivating a whole-systems view, a sense of the relationship between things, and an integrative design sensibility. Similarly, the work of Bill Mollison on permaculture, including the basic permaculture textbooks and the *Introduction to Permaculture* (Tyalgum, Australia: Tagari Publications, 1991) while focused on creating sustainable human environments, cultivates systems thinking and integration skills.

George Leonard's book *Mastery* (New York: The Penguin Group, 1992) is a wonderful guide to cultivating mastery, and I highly recommend great teachers in timeless arts (e.g., martial arts, dance, yoga, visual arts, spiritual, etc.) as guides to cultivating mastery and integration.

The Cluetrain Manifesto: The End of Business As Usual by Rick Levine, Christopher Locke, Doc Searls, and David Weinberger (New York: HarperCollins, 2001) celebrates the emergence of the Web-enabled, networked marketplace, with ninety-five simple and direct theses.

Ultimately, if you are cultivating the skills of Working for Good, almost every person, resource, and experience you encounter can provide some opportunity for learning, growth, and development. Thus an open mind and heart are the greatest tools for cultivating all of the skills of Working for Good.

ABOUT THE AUTHOR

Jeff Klein is the CEO of Cause Alliance Marketing®, an organization that designs and produces collaborative cause-related marketing programs that address social issues while fulfilling the business objectives of alliance partners. He currently serves as Executive Director and Chief Activation Officer for FLOW—a nonprofit dedicated to "liberating the entrepreneurial spirit for good" co-founded by John Mackey, CEO of Whole Foods Market, and educational entrepreneur Michael Strong. Jeff Klein was one of the visionaries and driving forces behind Private Music, the career of Yanni, Spinning, Seeds of Change, and Chi Running, and he has consulted for the Esalen Institute, the National Geographic Society, GlobalGiving, the Institute of Noetic Sciences, and more. For more information, visit causealliancemarketing.com.